Assessment-Centered Teaching

Assessment-Centered Teaching

A Reflective Practice

Kathryn DiRanna • Ellen Osmundson • Jo Topps • Lynn Barakos
Maryl Gearhart • Karen Cerwin • Diane Carnahan • Craig Strang

A Joint Publication

CORWIN PRESS
A SAGE Company
Thousand Oaks, CA 91320

For information:

Corwin Press
A SAGE Company
2455 Teller Road
Thousand Oaks, California 91320
www.corwinpress.com

SAGE India Pvt. Ltd.
B 1/I 1 Mohan Cooperative
  Industrial Area
Mathura Road, New Delhi 110 044
India

SAGE Ltd.
1 Oliver's Yard
55 City Road
London EC1Y 1SP
United Kingdom

SAGE Asia-Pacific Pte. Ltd.
33 Pekin Street #02–01
Far East Square
Singapore 048763

Printed in the United States of America.

Library of Congress Cataloging-in-Publication Data

Assessment-centered teaching : a reflective practice / Kathryn DiRanna . . . [et al.].
    p. cm.
Includes bibliographical references and index.
ISBN 978-1-4129-5462-4 (cloth)
ISBN 978-1-4129-5463-1 (pbk.)
   1. Teaching—Evaluation. 2. Effective teaching. 3. Reflective teaching.
I. DiRanna, Kathryn. I. Title.

LB1025.3.A85 2008
371.14′4—dc22   2007040294

This book is printed on acid-free paper.

08   09   10   11   12   10   9   8   7   6   5   4   3   2   1

Acquisitions Editor:	Dan Alpert
Editorial Assistant:	Tatiana Richards
Production Editor:	Eric Garner
Copy Editor:	Paula L. Fleming
Typesetter:	C&M Digitals (P) Ltd.
Proofreader:	Kevin Gleason
Indexer:	Sheila Bodell
Cover Designer:	Scott Van Atta

Contents

Resource B: *Assessment-Centered Teaching Portfolio* **Forms,
is located on the book's accompanying CD-ROM.**

Foreword

This book reflects our journey toward classroom assessment in the service of student learning. The journey commenced in the fall of 2001, when the National Science Foundation (NSF) funded our Center for the Assessment and Evaluation of Student Learning (CAESL), a multidisciplinary organization whose mission was to strengthen the design and use of assessment to improve student learning in science at all levels of the educational system. Our responsibility was to build science teachers' capacities to engage in formative assessment, and the NSF encouraged us to design new professional development strategies in collaboration with other CAESL experts. Our project brought together the diverse expertise of researchers, assessment specialists, psychometricians, curriculum developers, professional development leaders, and science teachers and administrators in a new community to address the critical issues around our mission. The products were our model of Assessment-Centered Teaching (ACT) together with the *Assessment-Centered Teaching Portfolio*, a reflective tool that supports teachers on their journey toward assessment in the service of student learning.

The phrase "Assessment-Centered Teaching" emerged from our commitment to assessment that is *integrated* with science teaching in ongoing cycles of planning, instruction, assessment, and revision of instruction. Teachers must not only assess what students understand, they must use that information systematically in their teaching to guide students toward sound understanding of science concepts and processes. Ongoing and systematic use of formative assessment is critical to reduce existing learning gaps among student populations. Our *Assessment-Centered Teaching Portfolio* was designed to deepen teachers' perspectives on student understanding and enhance and refine their pedagogical repertoires for teaching as well as for assessment.

Our professional development community crossed the traditional divide between researchers and practitioners, between academics and service providers, between those prone to observing and theorizing, and those inclined to action and its immediate realities. We worked hard to meld our perspectives, a process that was not always easy. In fact, truth be told, the process sometimes was quite frustrating! We experienced a clash of cultures as professionals with fundamentally different knowledge bases and norms of operation, journeying to create a joint vision of the integration of assessment, teaching, and learning and to bring that vision to reality through an engaging and feasible professional development program. Through respectful dialogue and problem solving, we were able to come together to design a process and product that prompted teachers to change their practices in meaningful ways.

We believe that the journey has enabled us to make important connections in what too often have been separate pathways of knowledge and practice. Our agenda was developed on the premise that classroom assessment practices are likely to have the largest payoffs in advancing student learning (Black, Harrison, Lee, Marshall, & Wiliam, 2003; Black & Wiliam, 1998a, 1998b). Yet we saw serious impediments to harnessing assessment's potential power (Herman, 1997; Plake & Impara, 1997; Stiggins, 2002). We aimed to address this gap through the advancement of a unique professional development program for teachers.

Our work commenced just as the National Research Council was releasing *Knowing What Students Know* (Pellegrino, Chudowsky, & Glaser, 2001), bringing together recent advances in cognitive and measurement science to suggest new foundations for educational assessment. Advocating the primacy of assessment to benefit student learning, *Knowing What Students Know* observed that

> . . . every assessment . . . rests on three pillars: a model of how students represent knowledge and develop competence in a subject matter domain; tasks or situations that allow one to observe students' performance; and an interpretation method for drawing inferences from the performance evidence thus obtained. (p. 2)

We took *Knowing What Students Know* deliberations as a starting point for defining quality assessment, leavened with the accepted standards of the field, the *Standards for Educational and Psychological Testing* (American Educational Research Association [AERA],

American Psychological Association [APA], and National Council for Measurement in Education [NCME], 1999) and its more traditional concepts of validity, reliability, and fairness; and we sought to define these concepts from the perspective of classroom assessment. We incorporated the research contributions of CAESL colleagues Rich Shavelson and Mark Wilson. Rich's work put front and center the notion of targeting assessments on specific types of knowledge and learning—declarative, procedural, schematic, and strategic—and provided specific templates for moving beyond the assessment of factual knowledge to complex thinking and problem solving (Shavelson, Ruiz-Primo, & Wiley, 2005). Mark's psychometric prowess advanced the notion of creating assessments that could track students' learning trajectories to provide teachers with information on whether and how students develop sophisticated understanding and competence in a discipline (Wilson, 2004).

We also well knew that quality assessment was only a part of the problem of quality assessment practices. If assessment was to benefit student learning, quality assessments needed to do more than just exist and be administered; the data from them needed to be *used* actively to promote learning. We thus added to the basic framework in *Knowing What Students Know* a model of assessment use and recognized that the assessment process needed to be developed and implemented hand-in-hand with plans for curriculum and instruction. Assessment could not be an add-on but rather needed to be an integral part of the pedagogical process.

We viewed quality assessment as an integrated system that could provide teachers with rich feedback for gauging and responding to student progress on desired learning goals throughout the instructional process. We were talking not only about an assessment process but an integrated instructional process. To accomplish this, we drew from three well-regarded instructional design models, including the 5E model (Bybee, 1997), the three-phase learning cycle (Atkin & Karplus, 1962; Karplus & Thier, 1967), and the backward design process (Wiggins & McTighe, 2005). In terms of professional development design, we adapted the *Professional Development Design Framework* from *Designing Professional Development for Teachers of Science and Mathematics* (Loucks-Horsley, Love, Stiles, Mundry, & Hewson, 2003) and endeavored to incorporate principles of adult learning (Knowles, Holton, & Swanson, 1998; National Staff Development Council, 2001), the conditions for transformative learning (Thompson & Zeuli, 1999), and the components of professional learning communities (Louis, Kruse, & Bryk, 1995).

It is worth noting that we tried to practice what we preached in terms of integrating assessment with learning. The *Assessment-Centered Teaching Portfolio*—which is a central tool in our professional development strategy of reflective practice—was initially developed as a research tool to gather data on whether and how participating teachers were developing assessment expertise and to define a trajectory of learning for teachers' assessment practices. Researchers' observations of teachers' progress provided ongoing feedback to the professional development enterprise. As the portfolios were adapted for professional development purposes, they directly involved teacher-learners in self-assessment of their knowledge and practices, and they stretched teachers to use the feedback formatively to strengthen subsequent action. Analysis of the portfolios provided direct feedback and critical data to the professional development team, enabling the team to improve the professional development design. The portfolios also served as a coaching tool in work with individual teachers and were a centerpiece for collaborative reflection on practice.

We are proud of the progress we have made and hope that our experiences and lessons learned will be of benefit to others who are seeking to improve the practice of teaching and learning. At the same time, we recognize the limits of what we've been able to accomplish. Others have well expressed what we currently feel:

A journey of a thousand miles must begin with a single step. (Lao Tzu)

Success is never final. (Winston Churchill)

Our community and its journey continue. We invite you to join us.

—Joan L. Herman
CRESST/UCLA

Acknowledgments

We want to acknowledge all the teacher leaders of the CAESL professional development project whose participation in this learning community made our book possible. It is because of their hard work and dedication to student learning that we were inspired to create this guide to leading teachers in reflective practice and assessment. We want especially to thank the following teachers who contributed their work products to serve as examples in the book: Sylvia Brown, Rick Besocke, Deanne Clary, Khushwinder Gill, Sylvia Gutman, Frank Lucero, Mark McKay, Jeanne Ostrand, Becky Reid, Melissa Smith, and Cece Vevoda-Bible. Thanks also to the following school districts for their participation: Lake Elsinore Unified School District, Montebello Unified School District, San Diego Unified School District, Tracy Unified School District, and Vista Unified School District.

We thank the members of the CAESL research team led by Joan Herman—Sam Nagashima, Jennifer Pfotenhauer, Cheryl Schwab, and Terry Vendlinski—who helped to conduct teacher interviews and observations and aided in the collection and analysis of the teacher portfolios. We thank Steve Schneider and Mike Timms from the CAESL central office and the entire CAESL management team—Alicia Alonzo, Jacquey Barber, Joan Herman, Rich Shavelson, and Mark Wilson—for their leadership and guidance throughout the project. Their creative thinking in the development of the CAESL *Framework for Quality Assessment* has been pivotal for us in leading teachers in quality assessment practices.

We want to give special thanks to our colleague, Kathy Comfort, for helping to write the professional development component of the CAESL proposal and helping to implement our first year; to Catherine Halversen for working with us in delivering the first year of professional development; and to the National Science Foundation–funded Math Science Partnership professional development team, led by Vicki May at Washington University in St. Louis, for partnering with us to engage in still more in-depth work around assessment with teachers.

We want to give a very special thanks to Susan Mundry, whose patient guidance throughout our "writing a book" journey and insightful suggestions helped us to create coherency from the various contributions of our expansive writing team; to Kathy Stiles for her careful read and helpful comments that brought clarity to the text; to Deanna Maier for her most thorough work at creating the actual manuscript; to Jon Somers, a delightful graphic artist who did a marvelous job of translating words into pictures; to Dan Alpert at Corwin Press who guided our process and Paula Fleming who copyedited our work with style and precision; and to Doris Waters, whose skill at dealing with one hundred "emergencies" is unsurpassed. And, finally, we thank our colleagues and families for enduring our overtaxed schedules and frequent cross-state travel during the five years of this project.

Corwin Press would like to acknowledge the contributions of the following reviewers:

Kim Noble Beiderman
DCIU Staff Development
    Specialist
Holmes, PA

Jacie Bejster
Principal
Crafton Elementary
Pittsburgh, PA

Kathy Grover
Director of Curriculum
Clever R-V Schools
Springfield, MO

Page Keeley
Senior Science Program Director
Maine Mathematics and
    Science Alliance
Augusta, ME

Nancy Kellogg, PhD
Science Education Consultant
Boulder, CO

Harold Pratt
Educational Consultants Inc.
Littleton, CO

Marti Richardson
Executive Director
Tennessee Staff Development
    Council
Knoxville, TN

Jim Short, Ed.D.
Science Curriculum Coordinator
Denver Public Schools
Denver, CO

Rick Stiggins
Assessment Training Institute
Portland, OR

CAESL Professional Development Participants

Cynthia Angell
Richard Besocke
Peggy Blush
Sylvia Brown
Autumn Chapman
Deanne Clary
Ray Conser
Richard Dibler
Phyllis Duarte
Danine Ezell
Khushwinder (Kaur) Gill
Glenda Golobay
Kathy Green
Sylvia Gutman
Melissa Hamilton
Rya Hege
Diane Kelsey

Frank Lucero
Donna Markey
Mark McKay
Jzaron Mercer
Arturo Navar
Jeanne Ostrand
Mitchell Paik
Yvonne Pasinato
Marisa Ramirez
Bonnie Schindler
Melissa Smith
Juliette Solis
Larry Tallman
Cece Vevoda-Bible
Wayne Watanuki
Don Whisman
Tammy Wu

About the Authors

Kathryn DiRanna is the statewide director of WestEd's K–12 Alliance science professional development program and served as coleader of the CAESL Professional Development strand. She served as a PI/Project Director for the NSF-funded California Systemic Initiative and served on many state committees. Nationally, she was the mentor coordinator for the National Academy for Science and Mathematics Education Leadership, co–project director for the BSCS/WestEd National Academy for Curriculum Leadership, and codeveloper for the TERC/WestEd Using Data Project's professional development program. She has been a featured speaker at state and national conferences and served as the Program Coordinator for NSTA's National Convention. Kathy coauthored *Making Connections; The Science Assessment Facilitator Guide; The Guide to Selecting and Purchasing Instructional Materials;* and *The Data Coach's Guide to Improving Learning for All: Unleashing the Power of Collaborative Inquiry.* Kathy has received the California Science Teachers Association's Margaret Nicholson Award for Distinguished Service to Science Education and the Paul D. Hood Award from WestEd for distinguished service to the field.

Ellen Osmundson, PhD, is a senior researcher for the National Center for Research on Evaluation, Standards, and Student Testing (CRESST) at UCLA. Ellen served as a CAESL researcher working with the CAESL professional development team in addition to participating in other CAESL research. She has been a teacher, professional developer, and researcher on a wide variety of projects. She publishes and presents at national, state, and local conferences. Her research interests include cognition, learning and instruction, assessment, and reform education issues. Ellen is currently involved with CRESST work on the Assessment and Accountability Comprehensive Center, a project that focuses on implementing, evaluating, and improving state and local assessment and accountability systems.

Jo Topps is a regional director for WestEd's K–12 Alliance servicing Los Angeles and Orange counties in California. In her position, Jo directs the development, coordination, and implementation of professional development programs, kindergarten through postsecondary, on a regional, statewide, and national basis. Jo is a member of the CAESL professional development team. She has served on many state committees for science education and has served as a codeveloper for BSCS/WestEd's National Academy for Curriculum Leadership, professional developer for the TERC/WestEd Using Data Project, and mentor for the National Academy for Science and Mathematics Education Leadership. Jo coauthored *The Science Assessment Facilitator Guide* and *The Guide to Selecting and Purchasing Instructional Materials* and contributed to *Making Connections.* Jo is also a lecturer and supervisor of K–12 student teachers at California State University—Long Beach. She has presented at major national and state science and professional development conferences.

Lynn Barakos is a professional development specialist working in the Teacher Leadership Programs Department, the Center for Assessment and Evaluation of Student Learning (CAESL), and the Great Explorations in Math and Science (GEMS) programs at the Lawrence Hall of Science at the University of California, Berkeley. Lynn is a member of the CAESL professional development team as well as the CAESL Public Outreach team. She has taught and designed chemistry programs for children from preschool to high school, developed and presented extensive teacher education programs in science and inquiry, and consulted with teachers and districts about standards-based science education reform. She has actively participated in the GEMS Leaders and Associates network expansion, leading workshops both nationally and internationally.

Her current focus is on leading the assessment development team for GEMS' new science and literacy program called *Seeds of Science/Roots of Reading*.

Maryl Gearhart is adjunct associate professor in the Graduate School of Education, University of California, Berkeley, and a former senior researcher with CRESST at UCLA. Maryl served as a CAESL researcher working with the CAESL professional development team. Trained as a developmental psychologist, she focuses her teaching and research on strategies that help teachers interpret the ways students think and learn. She teaches graduate and undergraduate courses with a focus on elementary education, and she conducts research and publishes on a range of issues, including the effectiveness of professional development strategies, classroom practices in elementary mathematics, and portfolio assessment of writing.

Karen Cerwin is a regional director for WestEd's K–12 Alliance in Riverside and San Bernardino counties in California and served as a member of the CAESL professional development team. As a regional director, Karen is responsible for designing and implementing a variety of long-term science and mathematics professional development efforts in California. Her national experiences include providing technical assistance to the Curriculum Topic Study program, serving as a fellow in the National Academy for Science and Mathematics Education Leadership, codeveloping BSCS/WestEd's National Academy for Curriculum Leadership, and serving as a professional development provider for the TERC/WestEd Using Data Project. Karen was a contributing author to *The Science Assessment Facilitator's Guide* and *The Guide to Selecting and Purchasing Instructional Materials*. She is a frequent presenter at the National Staff Development Conference as well as the National Science Teacher's Association Conference.

Diane Carnahan is a regional director for WestEd's K–12 Alliance serving the Bay Area and San Joaquin Valley in California and served as a member of the CAESL professional development team. As a regional director for the K–12 Alliance, Diane directs the development, coordination, and implementation of science and math professional development programs, including being project director for two California Math and Science Partnership grants. She has been an educator for more than 20 years as an elementary teacher, county office science coordinator for the TOPS program working with retired scientists and schools, and adjunct professor at University of the Pacific for science methods classes. Diane has a strong emphasis in literacy, having served on the California Department of Education's science and literacy task force and having been the project director for Literacy in Science Academy (LISA), a collaboration with WestEd's Strategic Literacy Initiative. She is an invited speaker at state and national conferences.

Craig Strang is associate director of Lawrence Hall of Science (LHS) at the University of California, Berkeley. He is coleader of the CAESL Professional Development strand. Craig is the founding director of Marine Activities, Resources & Education (MARE), a K–8 professional development and curriculum development program focused on the integration of science and literacy. He is the lead principal investigator of the multi-institution, NSF-funded Center for Ocean Sciences Education Excellence—California. He received the National Marine Educators Association Marine Education Award in 2005 and coled the development of *Ocean Literacy: The Essential Principles of Ocean Sciences Grades K–12.* He is coauthor of three sets of K–8 science instructional materials: *Proyecto SOL: Science Oriented Learning, Project OCEAN,* and *MARE.* He is also coauthor of three teacher guides published by the LHS Great Explorations in Math and Science (GEMS) program. Craig has conducted field research on elephant seals and humpback whales and occasionally leads natural history eco-tours to Baja California and Galapagos.

Introduction

This book is not about testing. At least not the type of testing that we conduct at the end of the year to determine whether or not students are below basic or whether or not their schools should be categorized as low performing. Much is being written, mostly in the media, about that type of high-stakes testing. Instead, this book is about a different type of assessment for which we believe the stakes are even higher. It is about "quality classroom assessment," which is at the center and the heart of quality teaching, not merely at the end of it. The stakes are the essence of a quality education: equitable opportunities for all students to improve their understanding and become exceptional citizens of the world.

Our purpose in writing this book is to share the work, findings, and lessons learned from a National Science Foundation–funded National Center for Learning and Teaching program focused on assessment in science. The Center for Assessment and Evaluation of Student Learning (CAESL) is a collaborative partnership of WestEd, the University of California, Berkeley's Lawrence Hall of Science and Graduate School of Education, the University of California, Los Angeles's National Center for Research on Evaluation and Student Standards (CRESST), and Stanford University. Among many activities (research, new graduate programs, public understanding, preservice education), CAESL has been engaged in developing new strategies and tools to help K–12 teachers to build their knowledge and practice in student assessment. Through collaboration among professional developers, educational researchers, and practicing teachers, we developed tools and processes that assist teachers to become reflective practitioners through Assessment-Centered Teaching (ACT).

Assessment-Centered Teaching is the unique practice that occurs when teachers recognize assessment and instruction as integral to each other to improve student learning. It provides teachers with the information they need to understand what their students know;

the diverse ways in which students construct their understanding of concepts; how small, barely noticeable alternative conceptions might build into tenacious and persistent alternative conceptions; and most importantly, how teachers can reflect on, modify, and improve their curriculum and instruction to improve student learning. Assessment-Centered Teaching also provides students with a deeper understanding of their learning and makes them participants and partners in improving and deepening their conceptual understanding of complex ideas.

With the increased focus on assessment and accountability brought about by the 2001 No Child Left Behind Act, many educators have begun to examine data and student work. However, in all too many cases, once they identify a student's learning problem, their interventions often are superficial. School districts are applying "quick fixes" that offer little more than a possible bump in the test score and, too often, end up with the same problem the fix was designed to remedy—underperforming students. This cycle of ineffective remediation must be broken and replaced with an effective alternative. In this book, *Assessment-Centered Teaching: A Reflective Practice,* we offer such an alternative.

We describe new methods and approaches to help teachers build their expertise with assessment practice. Our core professional development strategy is the reflective *Assessment-Centered Teaching Portfolio,* a set of tasks that guide teachers through a process of planning, using, and revising classroom assessment for an instructional unit. Using the portfolio's prompts, teachers systematically examine student learning over time and monitor the development of students' conceptual understanding, guided by an instructional road map based on student learning goals. In this cycle of assessment and instruction, where evidence from assessment is used to inform learning goals, guide instruction, and revise assessments, *all* assessment becomes formative.

This book provides a realistic picture of what it takes to build a culture of ongoing assessment and reflective practice in the real world of teaching. Prior to our work, few professional development programs guided teachers to use quality assessment and reflect on student learning. Our book describes a coherent professional development model for building assessment-centered classrooms through teachers' reflective practices. The model includes innovative tools and processes developed from the current knowledge base and what we know about best practices for student assessment, teaching, teacher professional development, and teacher leadership.

Throughout this book, a story unfolds of dedicated teachers swimming upstream, doing their best to strive for genuine learning against a fast-moving current that pushes only for increased test scores. We recognize that teaching is increasingly more challenging and complex. Institutional, societal, and economic barriers compel teachers to teach more and more content each year with little regard to whether their students understand it. Yet our teachers continue to provide high-quality teaching and learning. The context of our professional development work has challenged and humbled both the researchers and professional developers but has, every day, heightened our appreciation and admiration of the work that teachers do with children and youth.

Through writing this book, we share the many lessons learned as the authors developed and implemented the Assessment-Centered Teaching model, including what it means to design and conduct transformative professional development (Thompson & Zeuli, 1999), the challenges and pitfalls faced, and the successes achieved in the project. The book also provides ideas and suggestions so that readers can use these lessons in their context.

Audience

Our book addresses the needs of a wide variety of educational practitioners interested in helping themselves and others to improve assessment and instructional practices. Professional developers and preservice educators will appreciate the tools and processes that promote teacher reflection and build teachers' capacities with Assessment-Centered Teaching. Teachers and administrators can learn new methods of planning, implementing, and revising classroom assessments from our description of the *Assessment-Centered Teaching Framework* and portfolio tasks as well as from case examples throughout the book. Curriculum developers will be introduced to ways that one tool, the Conceptual Flow, may be used to strengthen the coherence of instructional materials. Researchers will be intrigued by ways that Academy researchers, professional developers, and school practitioners worked together to design a process of reflective practice to strengthen classroom assessment. All readers will be interested in the accounts of teacher change that provide a vision of teachers as professionals engaged in lifelong learning.

Our work focuses on developing teacher assessment practice in the science classroom. We purposefully chose this discipline because, on a nationwide basis, little attention is paid to the teaching and learning of science in comparison to literacy or mathematics. However, we believe that teachers and educators in any discipline can successfully use the processes and tools described throughout this book.

Organization of the Book

Building on the idea that "assessment and learning are two sides of the same coin" (National Research Council, 2001, p. 5), Assessment-Centered Teaching recognizes that assessment and instruction are two sides of the same coin: the coin—the object of value—is student learning. The opening chapters introduce the reader to our foundational thinking about the integration of assessment and instruction, reflection, and the importance of collaborative work. Ensuing chapters depict each of the parts of the *Assessment-Centered Teaching Portfolio* and the processes we used to facilitate teacher reflection. Each of the portfolio chapters answers the following guiding questions: How does the tool relate to the *Assessment-Centered Teaching Framework?* What is the tool and its purpose? How is the tool used to build reflective practice? How does the tool bring about changes in teacher practice? We also embed questions from the *Assessment Centered Teaching Portfolio* that encourage teachers to reflect on their practice. The closing chapters summarize our learning.

Throughout all of the chapters, we draw on teachers' voices to explain the use of the *Assessment-Centered Teaching Portfolio* and the impact of reflection on their practice. We also provide several teacher cases to engage the reader with transformative changes in teaching practice. The examples used in the chapters are not intended as exemplars. Instead, they represent the thinking of teachers who are becoming assessment-centered teachers.

Chapter 1 introduces our point of view: assessment and instruction are integral to each other. This chapter describes the theory of action that guided the design of our strategies for supporting teachers on their journey to assessment-centered teaching. We introduce the *Assessment-Centered Teaching Framework,* the professional development design, and our core strategy, the *Assessment-Centered Teaching Portfolio,* to provide context for ensuing chapters. Chapter 1 concludes with the story of one teacher, Yvette Jones, to illustrate the transformations in teacher practice that can emerge when teachers embrace Assessment-Centered Teaching.

Chapter 2 describes the *Assessment-Centered Teaching Framework.* The framework elements include assessment knowledge that we represent in the Assessment Knowledge Triangle, assessment practice, and the relationship of both to instruction in the Assessment-Instruction Cycle. This chapter captures the foundational thinking that is critical for teachers as they develop the habits of Assessment-Centered Teaching.

Chapter 3 discusses the importance of reflective practice for professional growth and ongoing instructional improvement. We present our reflective practice strategy, the *Assessment-Centered Teaching Portfolio*, to acquaint the reader with the rationale for the strategy before reading the details and impact of its use in Chapters 4–10.

Chapters 4, 5, and 6 discuss the beginning of the Assessment-Instruction Cycle in which teachers plan for assessment and instruction. Chapter 4 describes how to establish goals for student learning by constructing a Conceptual Flow. Chapter 5 discusses the use of the Record of Assessment in Instructional Materials (RAIM) for designing an assessment plan based on the Conceptual Flow. Chapter 6 describes ways to promote teacher reflection about the assessment plan before instruction, including selecting target students for analysis of student work and considering pitfalls of student understanding to inform instruction.

Chapters 7 and 8 describe how to guide assessment-centered teachers as they interpret the student work they gathered from their implemented assessment plan. The student work serves as evidence of student learning, and analysis of the work is the basis for making revisions to instruction and assessment practices. Chapter 7 describes the criteria for scoring student work, while Chapter 8 discusses the analysis of patterns in student responses for both whole class and target students.

Chapters 9 and 10 discuss how assessment-centered teachers use the evidence from student work. In Chapter 9, we explain how the portfolio guides teachers to use assessment information to revise their instruction and provide feedback to students. Chapter 10 discusses the ways that the portfolio supports teachers as they use evidence to revise their assessment tool, both the tasks and the scoring criteria.

Chapter 11 describes our professional development design based on the *Professional Development Design Framework* from *Designing Professional Development for Teachers of Science and Mathematics* (Loucks-Horsley et al., 2003) so that others might consider our design in their context.

Chapter 12 uses the five requirements for transformative learning (Thompson & Zeuli, 1999, pp. 355–357) as a framework for our discussion of lessons learned. We include applications of the portfolio process to other contexts and share our reflections.

Resource A provides a list of additional readings on assessments, student alternative conceptions, and professional development.

The enclosed CD-ROM (Resource B) contains the *Assessment-Centered Teaching Portfolio* forms that teachers used to guide their work and their reflection. These forms can be used as black line masters, if desired.

Navigation Guide

While we would like the reader to know our entire story by reading every chapter, we know that some of the topics have greater utility than others for specific contexts. The following suggestions will help readers navigate our work:

- Readers interested in reflective practice as a professional development strategy should read all chapters, concentrating on Chapter 3 and the questions concerning building reflective practice and changes in teacher practice in Chapters 4–10.
- If interested in how to plan for assessment and instruction, read Chapters 4, 5, and 6.
- Readers interested in specific planning tools, such as the Conceptual Flow and the Record of Assessment in Instructional Materials (RAIM), should read Chapters 4 and 5.
- If interested in how to select and plan for assessment, read Chapter 5.
- Readers interested in how to interpret student work should read Chapters 7 and 8.
- Readers interested in how to use evidence from student work to improve instruction and assessment should read Chapters 9 and 10.
- If interested in our professional development design, transformative learning, and lessons learned, read Chapters 11 and 12.
- Read Chapter 12 for applications to other contexts and our reflections.
- If interested in the *Assessment-Centered Teaching Portfolio* forms, see the enclosed CD-ROM.

1

Building the Foundation

Let's start at the very beginning, a very nice place to start. When you read you begin with A-B-C. When you sing you begin with do-re-mi.

—Rodgers and Hammerstein*

When you teach, you begin with assessment! This novel idea, a paradigm shift in the way most teachers think about teaching and learning, was the foundation of a new approach to professional development design for the Center for the Assessment and Evaluation of Student Learning (CAESL) funded by the National Science Foundation (NSF) from 2001 to 2006. From our prior work in professional development and school reform throughout the country, we knew that teachers value the idea that alignment between curriculum, instruction, and assessment leads to better student understanding, as illustrated in Figure 1.1. We had long observed, however, that teachers' knowledge and beliefs can change before they are translated into practice. This lag in implementation can be especially pronounced for use of assessment, perhaps because teachers, professional developers,

Figure 1.1   Alignment for Student Understanding

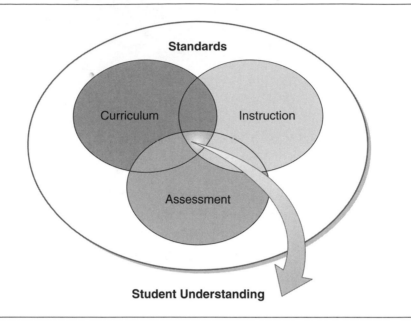

curriculum developers, and instructional leaders lack the theoretical underpinnings and the practical tools to put their knowledge and beliefs about assessment into action. Many teachers focus on only two of the circles seen in Figure 1.1—curriculum and instruction—while assessment "just happens," usually as an afterthought and almost always for the purpose of grading.

In 2001, we developed a different vision of teaching and learning in classrooms. Our vision was built on the view of assessment originally expressed in the *National Science Education Standards:* "Assessment and learning are two sides of the same coin" (National Research Council [NRC], 1996, p. 5). In our professional development program, *assessment* and *instruction* were two sides of the same coin, and the coin—the object of value—was student learning. That vision became the foundation of our work and the basis for this book. Our vision includes classrooms in which teachers do the following:

- Think about assessment and their goals for student learning at the beginning, middle, and end of instructional units.
- Guide their instruction toward explicit learning goals, monitoring how students progress in their understandings of the targeted concepts.

- Faithfully and routinely use student work to understand what their students understand and adjust their instructional design and teaching accordingly.

In other words, we envisioned *Assessment-Centered Teaching*. Our goal was to create professional development experiences, tools, and, importantly, a framework that, taken together, assist teachers in making the integral relationship between instruction and assessment a reality in their classrooms.

Theory of Action

Throughout our work, we have embraced the classroom vision of the *National Science Education Standards:* students at all grade levels engaged in understanding important scientific concepts through inquiry-based investigations (NRC, 1996). Implementing this vision requires that teachers have a reasonably deep understanding of science, knowledge of how students reason and learn ("pedagogical content knowledge," Shulman, 1986), and expertise with assessment to develop assessment methods and interpret student understanding in sound and valid ways (Shepard, 2001). We knew that our professional development program needed to include an equal focus on the importance of understanding science content to identify appropriate learning goals and on identifying the range of understandings that students have about particular science concepts.

Our theory of action included the assumption that long-term professional development combined with ongoing reflective practice is required to effect any significant change in teachers' practices. We wanted to avoid the "halo" effect of many other professional development programs in which participants leave "talking reform talk" but are unable to implement reform in their classroom (Weiss, 1997).

Thus, our theory of action guided us toward the development of three program components: 1) an *Assessment-Centered Teaching (ACT) Framework* that integrates sound instruction and assessment practice in the service of student learning, 2) a professional development program design built on the *ACT Framework* that emphasizes teacher collaboration and transformative learning, and 3) the *Assessment-Centered Teaching Portfolio* linked to the framework as a strategy to guide teachers' reflection about their practice. In this chapter, we provide an overview of these components to underscore the assumptions, ideas, tools, and processes that form the content of this book.

Assessment-Centered Teaching Framework

We turned to theory and research on sound instruction and classroom assessment as we designed the framework. We found that formative assessment must be an essential component of Assessment-Centered Teaching. The evidence is clear that ongoing assessment by teachers, combined with appropriate feedback to students, produces strong positive effects on achievement. In their review of research on the impact of classroom assessment on student learning, Black and Wiliam (1998a, 1998b) documented the power of formative assessment for supporting student learning. From more than 200 studies, they selected 20 that were rigorous in their methods and reported that

> all of these studies show that innovations, which include strengthening the practice of formative assessment, produce significant and often substantial learning gains. These studies range over ages (from 5-year-olds to university undergraduates), across several school subjects and over several countries. (1998b, p. 139)

We also found that sound instructional practices include purposeful planning of learning sequences based on the information gained from formative assessment. One such example of purposeful planning is the 5E instructional model (Bybee, 1997). Based on the learning cycle developed by Atkin and Karplus in the 1960s, the 5E instructional model provides multiple opportunities for teachers to assess student understanding throughout a learning sequence and thus make instructional decisions based on this information (Atkin & Karplus, 1962; Karplus & Thier, 1967).

Our goal was to integrate assessment throughout instructional planning and implementation, and we decided the way to do that was to keep teachers' instructional materials at the center of the work. If teachers learn to plan assessments as they plan their instructional units, they will learn to view assessment and instruction as a cycle in which evidence from assessment guides instruction to ensure that students

Chapter 2 contains a complete description of the *Assessment-Centered Teaching Framework.* Figure 1.2 is a summary of the *Framework.*

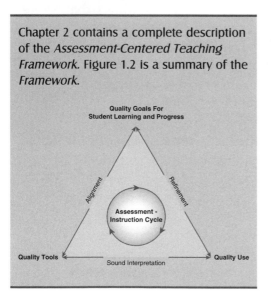

Quality Goals For
Student Learning and Progress

Alignment

Refinement

Assessment -
Instruction Cycle

Quality Tools

Sound Interpretation

Quality Use

make progress toward the learning goals. Evidence from assessments will also inform the revision of assessments for use in future implementations of the unit. In this way, all assessment is formative, including the traditional tests that come at the end of the chapter. Through repeated cycles of assessment planning, implementation, and revision, teachers can reflect on the results of key assessments and their implications for improving instruction and student learning of science concepts.

We expected that Assessment-Centered Teaching would represent a major change in thinking for most teachers, and we developed the *Assessment-Centered Teaching Framework* to communicate our new ideas clearly to teachers. This framework is the theoretical basis of our work. The triangle represents fundamental elements of *assessment knowledge*, such as the characteristics of quality goals for student learning and progress, quality tools (both assessment tasks and scoring guides), and quality use of evidence, and it portrays the relationships among these elements. But strengthening teachers' knowledge is not enough to impact teacher practice, and thus the framework also includes the Assessment-Instruction Cycle to depict what is involved in using quality assessment practices from planning, to instruction, to revision of classroom assessments. The *Assessment-Centered Teaching Framework* represents our vision for teachers, and we designed professional development experiences around teachers' instructional units so their learning would be directly relevant to their practices.

Professional Development Program Design

To guide teachers in the development of Assessment-Centered Teaching, we designed a professional development program built on the *ACT Framework* and based on the principles of effective and transformative teacher learning (Loucks-Horsley, Love, Stiles, Mundry, & Hewson, 2003; Thompson & Zeuli, 1999). Our program, called the Science Assessment Leadership Academy, included many authentic opportunities for collaboration and transformative learning and provided the infrastructure for community building. In our Academy model, district teams comprised of K–12 teachers and an administrator participated for three

A detailed explanation of the professional development program design is found in Chapter 11. We explain how we used the Professional Development Design Framework (Loucks-Horsley et al., 2003) to guide the design and implementation of the Academy. We also used the five principles of transformative learning recommended by Thompson and Zeuli (1999) and, in Chapter 12, reflect on their use in summarizing what we learned about effective professional development from the Academy experience.

years. The last two years focused on using classroom assessment, the emphasis of this book. The year-round Academy consisted of statewide meetings and on-site implementation. Statewide meetings were scheduled as 5-day institutes in the summer and two 3-day seminars during the school year. On-site implementation sessions were conducted in classrooms as well as in meetings at school or district sites.

Our premise that teachers build knowledge and strengthen practice through collaboration is grounded in research. Teachers improve their methods of formative assessment when they work with colleagues, professional developers, and/or researchers to design actual assessments that reveal student thinking in the course of daily practice (Atkin & Coffey, 2003). This type of reflective practice is even more powerful in collegial settings (Osterman & Kottkamp, 2004) where thinking by both teachers and students is made public and instructional practice is deprivatized (Hord, 1998; Little, Gearhart, Curry, & Kafka, 2003).

We offered a variety of opportunities for collaboration on authentic tasks. During statewide meetings, all participants worked together in activities designed to build their knowledge of methods to develop quality goals for student learning and progress, quality assessment tools, and quality uses of assessments. But the core strategy was the creation of grade-level teams, who worked together to strengthen assessments for common reform-based instructional materials in science and document their work in the *Assessment-Centered Teaching Portfolio* (described below).

> Examples of the reform instructional materials used in the Academy are listed in Chapter 11.

Each member of these teams was highly motivated to improve their practices, and the collaboration provided the excitement of sharing and developing new ideas. Teachers then returned to their classrooms to teach the unit and gather and score student work individually. When they reconvened with their team at the next state meeting, they shared the student work in their portfolios, analyzed patterns and trends, and planned revisions in instruction and assessment based on their analyses.

Unit-alike teams continued to work on the same reform-based unit for two years. Repeating the unit and continued sharing brought forth new insights from the teachers, particularly in planning for and noting students' alternative conceptions and struggles within a unit of instruction. Additionally, in the spring of each year, participants applied their use of the processes to their district-adopted instructional units (some of which were also reform-based instructional materials, while others were traditional texts).

The Academy also included a leadership component. Guided by the *ACT Framework,* we designed a variety of common activities that district teams could use in their context. For example, at on-site meetings, teachers and administrators met to develop plans for sharing what they were learning with district colleagues. The team used professional development modules from our program (e.g., developing Conceptual Flows or looking at student work) to facilitate faculty learning or facilitate the beginning of assessment study groups. In addition, the statewide meetings provided a venue for district teams to share how they were disseminating the *ACT Framework* and strategies and to network and problem solve.

Assessment-Centered Teaching Portfolio

Perhaps most importantly, our theory of action incorporated reflection in every activity. We wanted teachers to make decisions as reflective practitioners—to use their reflections to "act in a deliberate, intentional manner" to improve student learning (Reagan, Case, & Brubacher, 2000). We wanted teachers to make these decisions by drawing upon their knowledge of science, developmentally appropriate curriculum, instructional strategies, and assessment practices.

Our centerpiece strategy for building Assessment-Centered Teaching is the *Assessment-Centered Teaching Portfolio,* a reflective tool that translates the *ACT Framework* into practice and supports teachers as they integrate instruction and assessment. The portfolio is a series of prompts that addresses planning for assessment and instruction, analyzing student work, and using evidence from student work to guide instruction and revising assessments. The portfolio's tools and processes support individual and collaborative reflection, both written and oral. A teacher can use the portfolio for reflection "in the moment," noting ideas about the quality of assessment items, student understanding, or revisions for instruction. At Academy meetings, team members shared their ideas in a collaborative setting. Our community provided ample opportunities for teachers to reflect on, examine, and challenge current practice to bring about transformational change in assumptions and beliefs about teaching, learning, and assessment.

The *Assessment-Centered Teaching Portfolio,* its process and tools and impact on teacher practice, is the focus of this book. In Chapters 3–10, we describe the portfolio tools and process in detail and explain how the reflective process helped teachers fully integrate assessment and instruction.

Results of the Portfolio Experience: Yvette's Story

The goals of the Science Assessment Leadership Academy were challenging, and its design was complex. Yet the expertise and spirit of the teacher leaders, professional developers, and researchers yielded notable breakthroughs for each; and for many, the changes were transformational. None of us will look at assessment and instruction in quite the same way again. To illustrate the transformations we observed in teachers' orientations to assessment, we introduce Yvette Jones, a veteran middle school science and mathematics teacher who participated in the Academy with her district team for three years. Yvette's story is about a transformation in one teacher's stance toward assessment, from summative tests for assigning grades to formative assessments that guided improvements in her instruction. As Yvette comments,

> [Working on the portfolio] has given me an opportunity to look at how I teach and how I examine the student work—not just to assess students, but to assess the lesson and what's effective and what's not effective. . . . Whereas before it was, "OK. I have a test. I need to give it." . . . Now I realize, it doesn't have to end with a final grade—[the assessment] can be something that helps me to structure my lessons. . . . to gauge students' progress over time throughout the unit . . . [and to] strategically plan to optimize learning for all of my students.

Through her work with the Academy and the *Assessment-Centered Teaching Portfolio,* Yvette took professional ownership of her instructional materials. She came to understand that Assessment-Centered Teaching required her to critique learning goals and assessment tools to ensure that they provided the formative information she needed to guide instruction and provide her students with valuable feedback.

Background

With 15 years of experience, Yvette Jones is a teacher committed to her students and to her ongoing development as a professional. During the Academy, Yvette was responsible for teaching three 6th-grade mathematics/science core classes in a suburban middle school that served students of diverse language backgrounds, ethnicities, and socioeconomic status. Over two years, Yvette completed three portfolios based on Great Explorations in Math and Science (GEMS) instructional materials. During Year 1, she taught two GEMS units,

Plate Tectonics: The Way the Earth Works (Cuff , 2002) and *Hot Water, Warm Homes.* In Year 2, she taught *Plate Tectonics: The Way the Earth Works* again, but with revisions she made to the unit. Equity was a driving principle in her work. Yvette was motivated to use the *Assessment-Centered Teaching Portfolio* to strengthen her assessment expertise so she could better support the learning of all students.

Yvette brought a great deal of background knowledge to the Academy. She had experience with science inquiry units as well as knowledge of the Conceptual Flow process: an approach for analyzing the scientific content of inquiry units and establishing learning goals (see Chapter 4). She had once collaborated in the design of performance tasks and rubrics for inquiry units, so she had some understanding of quality assessment tools. Perhaps the most relevant background was her experience with the K–12 Alliance/WestEd's Teaching Learning Collaborative (see Resources), a lesson study program that emphasizes informal formative assessment as well as backward design when planning and implementing lessons (Bybee, 1997; Wiggins & McTighe, 2005). In that project, she developed "decision point assessments" (DiRanna & Cerwin, 1994), informal strategies for gathering information on student understanding during lessons. From that project, she became intrigued by the role and value of formative assessment for supporting student learning, but she had no experience developing more formal and systematic assessments used for formative purposes throughout an instructional unit. Yvette immediately recognized the value of the Academy and the *Assessment-Centered Teaching Portfolio* process. She knew she would benefit from a context and a process for aligning learning goals, assessments, and instruction throughout an instructional unit to support student learning better.

What Yvette Learned

As we describe in Chapters 3 through 10, the *Assessment-Centered Teaching Portfolio* used by Yvette and the other Academy participants had multiple sections, including "Plan for Assessment-Instruction," "Analyze Student Work," "Use Evidence to Inform Instruction," and "Use Evidence to Refine Assessments." Yvette grew in remarkable ways from her work in each part of the portfolio, even as she faced some persistent challenges.

Plan for Assessment-Instruction. Assessment-Centered Teaching emphasizes the importance of unit *assessment planning* to establish clear learning goals and identify assessments for analyzing student progress toward those goals (see Chapters 4 and 5). Yvette had never designed an assessment plan for an instructional unit before her work in the Academy. It was a new idea to follow changes in student understanding from a pre-assessment linked through several juncture (interim) assessments to a post-assessment. It's hardly a surprise then that Yvette's initial assessment plan in her first portfolio was essentially a compilation of any assessments she and her colleagues could find in the *Plate Tectonics* unit. They weren't sure exactly what they were looking for and listed pages of unit activities that they felt had assessment potential. Many of these, however, were not well aligned with the core learning goals or with one another. By the time Yvette finished her third portfolio, she had developed a far more *strategic* and *integrated* approach to assessment planning, as she describes here:

> *Now I can see where a pretest for the entire unit is also valuable, and that you can use it to gauge students' progress over time throughout the unit. You can actually document a well-laid out map of the conceptual flow and base that on which concepts the students understood or didn't understand. [Using juncture assessments] gives you the opportunity to look back on student progress in a more strategic way and figure out where the pitfalls were for each concept for each lesson. And [the juncture] is considered a crucial place . . . [because] if students don't have understanding of certain concepts, they're not going to be able to fully connect concepts later on in the unit.*

   How did Yvette develop these insights? When Yvette and her colleagues analyzed the unit concepts for the third portfolio, they identified the key concepts to assess and thought about ways that later concepts build on prior concepts as students progress through the unit. Then, when they planned the assessments, they were prepared to document student progress accordingly. Instead of recording the learning goals in one document and a list of assessments in another document, Yvette and her colleagues represented their integrated curriculum and assessment plan in a single document, referred to as their "assessment plan," which they referenced throughout their teaching. She had come to understand that:

> *The pre-assessment, the post-assessment, and the juncture assessments actually pull the entire unit together and allow . . . me to chart student progress over time, and then, as a unit, be able to figure out where the pitfalls are in that unit.*

Analyze Student Work. Through careful analysis of sets of student work (Chapters 7 and 8), Yvette developed new methods of interpretation and a new understanding of assessment concepts that are critical to sound interpretation. She felt she grew most in this regard:

> *Having to look at the student work in detail is what's very different [about the ACT Portfolio process] and then documenting that and being able to use that documentation to look at student progress over time—it is definitely the biggest change in my practice.*

Beginning with her very first portfolio, Yvette learned a key lesson about assessment—that the information she could gain from student work was no better than the quality of her assessment tasks and assessment criteria. She very quickly shifted from acting as a consumer of her instructional materials to becoming a professional who took ownership of her materials and made revisions to the assessments as needed. Recognizing that assessments had to be aligned with instruction, she revised many of the assessment tasks in her first portfolio so that they targeted the concepts she had identified as her learning goals. She also revised the instructions for some tasks when she became aware that her students did not clearly understand the tasks. When she had time to reflect before she implemented an assessment, Yvette made changes to her tasks; but if she discovered weaknesses in her assessments after administration, she quickly devised a follow-up assessment and made revisions to the original tasks for future use.

Her growing commitment to quality assessment was also reflected in her methods of developing scoring criteria (see Chapter 7). When Yvette sat down with a set of student work, she always revised the draft criteria that she had sketched in her initial assessment plan. She reviewed student papers and refined the criteria to ensure that her scores captured the full range of her students' responses. As she comments:

> *I've learned how crucial it is to have a rubric . . . because you create a rubric and you're looking for some very specific answers . . . so having a rubric helped me to be consistent . . . I could see what the focused concepts were and give credit for that and not just, "Oh they tried to give their ideas." . . . The criteria . . . [have] to be based on concepts that you covered and . . . [must be] . . . detailed enough so that you're not making assumptions or inferences.*

Other arenas of growth were her methods of analyzing patterns and trends for the whole class and for target students (see Chapter 8). In her first portfolio, for example, Yvette omitted whole-class analysis for some assessments: "I had no strategic way of writing and recording everything." But in her second and third portfolios, she devised various ways to chart scores and examine patterns among items and students, and she began to cluster items that measured the same major concept.

Use Evidence to Guide Instruction. Yvette recognized early that information from her unit assessments was not only a crucial resource for improving her instruction but also a way to provide students with valuable feedback about their learning. She shared results with students because "[students] learn from the assessments." She began to share the pre-assessment results, because she recognized that they "give the students an understanding of where they're at" before she launched the unit. She also implemented targeted follow-up activities after key assessments to engage students more deeply with the concepts. For example, she often had students work collaboratively in small groups, record their discussions about concepts covered in the assessments on small whiteboards, and then share their reasoning with the whole class.

Use Evidence to Refine Assessments. Because Yvette recognized early that assessments often need refinement, she revised assessments frequently, and the revisions she documented in the final section of her portfolio represented only a small portion of her efforts. Noteworthy was her recognition that the quality of an assessment depends on its alignment with the targeted learning goals and the purpose for giving the assessment. When Yvette worked on an assessment, she reflected, "What do I really need to know about my students' understanding at this point?" Yvette became increasingly interested in assessments that revealed student conceptions of scientific ideas as opposed to those that simply captured right or wrong answers. To deepen her knowledge of the ways students develop understanding of these core science ideas, Yvette read materials suggested to her by Academy facilitators. For example:

I bought the book, Benchmarks for Science Literacy *[American Association for the Advancement of Science, 1993]. And I looked in it and thought, "OK, is this at grade level for these students?"—I saw that technically being able to discuss plate tectonics theory is not expected until about ninth through twelfth grade. So I thought, "OK, based on that, what should students [in sixth grade] understand?" I decided, based on standards and the Benchmarks[,] that students should understand that the Earth has convection currents that produce various types of volcanoes depending on the temperatures of the magma and different type of plate boundaries.*

She also discussed her insights about assessment tasks and criteria with her colleagues. Over time and in multiple contexts, Yvette developed more open-ended tasks aligned with the core science concepts in the unit, and she strengthened the criteria for scoring responses so her scores provided more information than just right or wrong answers.

Summary

Yvette Jones represents a teacher who used the *Assessment-Centered Teaching Portfolio* process to strengthen her assessment knowledge and practice and become an assessment-centered teacher. Through her portfolio work in individual and collaborative settings, Yvette came to recognize assessment as a formative way to monitor what her students understood and, through that process, to enable her to help all of her students to progress. What is most remarkable about Yvette's learning is that her growth cannot be isolated to one arena; she grew in many ways in her overall understanding of assessment principles and practices. Even more remarkable is that Yvette's growth in knowledge was reflected in immediate and measurable changes in her practice. She comments:

[I will take away from this experience] the way that I look at students' work, the way I will strategically grade students' work and give feedback, and the amount of time that goes into planning assessment. Enough time needs to be given to how students will take the test and then how you will grade the test and then how you will give feedback on their results from the test.

While Yvette learned all of the above and more, she also recognized that her learning was incomplete—and that recognition is the hallmark of a reflective practitioner. Yvette solidified her commitment to lifelong learning and ongoing professional development;

and she understood that a reflective practitioner continues to seek out resources and opportunities for collaboration throughout his or her teaching career.

> *I plan to continue to read resources such as* Classroom Assessment *and the* National Science Education Standards *[NRC, 2001], and collect student documentation formally and informally to analyze trends. [It is now] a common practice in my instruction. Staying involved in collaborative groups is key for me in the learning process.*

Yvette's learning illustrates the reflective, cyclical, and iterative ways that the *Assessment-Centered Teaching Portfolio* can guide improvements in all aspects of a teacher's instructional approach to science assessment.

2

Assessment-Centered Teaching

The premise of this book is that student learning can be enhanced through Assessment-Centered Teaching, and teachers can build Assessment-Centered Teaching through reflective practice. In this chapter, we present the key elements of Assessment-Centered Teaching, which include assessment knowledge, assessment practice, and the relationship of both to instruction.

What Is Assessment-Centered Teaching?

Ask teachers to describe their teaching practice, and their responses usually focus on the following: activities they use with their students; content they want their students to learn, often related to state standards; and instructional materials or other resources they use. The mention of assessment strategies tends to be absent from what they describe: very often assessment is, at best, an afterthought to instruction (Popham, 2008). If assessment is mentioned, teachers usually describe their struggles to cover what might be on a state test or how behind they are grading quizzes and end of chapter tests. Rarely is assessment mentioned as a critical element of instruction and the basis for instructional decisions.

Contrast the teachers above with our vision of the assessment-centered teacher. Assessment-centered teachers *always* mention assessment as an integral part of their teaching practice. They cannot think about instruction without considering the ways they use assessment tools and strategies to gather information about what students know and where instruction needs to go next.

Assessment-Centered Teaching is the result of combining best instructional practice and best assessment practice. It is founded on the principle that teachers need to integrate fully their knowledge of teaching with their knowledge of assessment to implement effective instructional decisions. Just as teachers rely upon their knowledge of content, teaching strategies, and instructional materials to plan and implement appropriate learning experiences, they must also rely on their knowledge of quality assessment practices to design sound methods of gathering information about student understanding. Assessment-centered teachers understand that, indeed, assessment and instruction are two sides of the same coin. To guide the paradigm shift toward Assessment-Centered Teaching, CAESL developed a framework for quality assessment, which our team of professional developers and researchers modified to create the *Assessment-Centered Teaching Framework.* As we saw in Chapter 1, Yvette was able to transform her understanding of assessment and her assessment practices through her Academy experiences. After three years of participation, implementation, and reflection, Yvette deeply understood the relationships among curriculum, instruction, and assessment; thus, her approach to assessment embodied a vision of the assessment-centered classroom.

Yvette's story illustrates the change we set out to create. Instead of focusing only on instruction, Yvette developed the habits of an assessment-centered teacher. What follows is the foundational thinking that enabled this shift in her knowledge and practice.

The *Assessment-Centered Teaching Framework*

Our professional development model helped teachers understand the knowledge base needed for quality instruction and assessment. While familiarity with this knowledge was important, it was not enough to transform teachers' assessment practices. Through our work with the researchers on our team, we began to recognize the interplay between assessment knowledge and practice and how reflection helps teachers bring assessment to the forefront of their thinking. The *Assessment-Centered Teaching Framework* (Figure 2.1) represents the collective work of CAESL researchers and practitioners trying to understand better the components of a quality classroom assessment system.

Figure 2.1   Assessment-Centered Teaching Framework

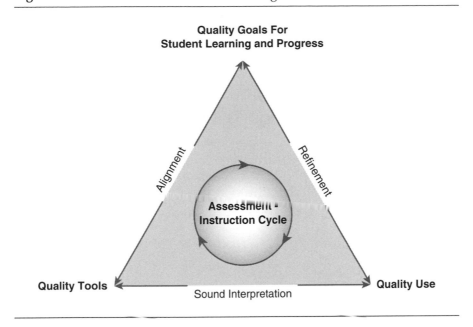

The *Assessment-Centered Teaching Framework* consists of two inter-related figures: the *Assessment Knowledge Triangle* and the *Assessment-Instruction Cycle*. The triangle represents the assessment knowledge we sought to strengthen in teachers. It consists of vertices labeled "Quality Goals for Student Learning and Progress," "Quality Tools," and "Quality Use" as well as bidirectional lines that indicate the alignments between vertices. The cycle in the center represents assessment practice and describes the relationship between engaging the students in instruction, assessing what happens and what is learned, and then re-engaging students in instruction based on evidence from the assessment. It represents what classroom practice looks like when teachers use Assessment-Centered Teaching.

The *Framework* also helps us understand the importance of alignment, not just among the knowledge vertices but also between the two key elements of Assessment-Centered Teaching: assessment knowledge (the triangle) and assessment practice (the cycle). To understand better these key elements, we provide a brief description of each and

> Current assessment practice addresses *formative assessment* as that which provides information about student learning during the course of instruction and *summative assessment* as that which measures students' progress at the end of a unit of instruction. In our view of assessment and instruction as a cycle, where evidence from assessments feeds back into learning goals, instruction, and assessment, *all* assessment is formative.

how assessment-centered teachers think about them. Both assessment knowledge and assessment practice continue to be addressed in detail throughout the book.

ACT Framework Expanded: Assessment Knowledge Triangle

Focusing first on the Assessment Knowledge Triangle, we discuss its vertices and describe the core assessment knowledge at each vertex (see Figure 2.2.). The three vertices include "Quality Goals for Student Learning and Progress," "Quality Tools," and "Quality Use."

Figure 2.2   *ACT Framework* Expanded Assessment Knowledge Triangle: Focus on Vertices

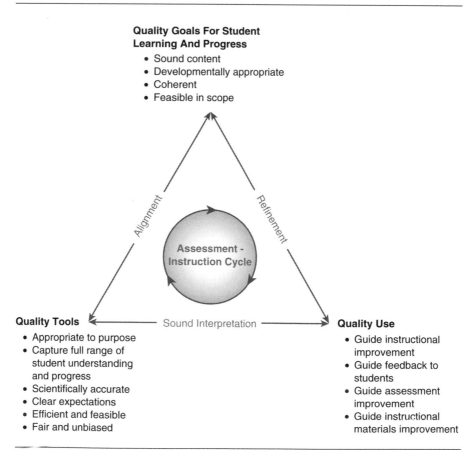

Quality Goals For Student Learning And Progress
- Sound content
- Developmentally appropriate
- Coherent
- Feasible in scope

Alignment

Refinement

Assessment - Instruction Cycle

Quality Tools   ← Sound Interpretation →   **Quality Use**

Quality Tools
- Appropriate to purpose
- Capture full range of student understanding and progress
- Scientifically accurate
- Clear expectations
- Efficient and feasible
- Fair and unbiased

Quality Use
- Guide instructional improvement
- Guide feedback to students
- Guide assessment improvement
- Guide instructional materials improvement

Quality Goals for Student Learning and Progress

There is a very close relationship between identifying (a) *what* students should know and be able to do and (b) *how* students will demonstrate that understanding. Therefore, assessment-centered teachers recognize that instructional unit planning entails three coordinated pieces: constructing learning goals, selecting the content to be taught, and selecting appropriate assessments.

Learning goals include content that is based on sound and accurate science and that is developmentally appropriate for the intended audience. For example, learning goals about the structure of an atom are more developmentally appropriate for secondary rather than elementary students. Coherent learning goals that sequence and link conceptual understanding for students help teachers decide what they want students to learn and when to assess student understanding along a learning trajectory. In addition, quality learning goals are feasible given the time and resources devoted to the identified concepts.

Quality Tools

Quality tools include both assessment tasks and scoring guides that are used to interpret student understanding. Quality tools are aligned to learning goals; selecting quality tools is as important as selecting quality instructional materials. Assessment-centered teachers understand that quality assessment tools have certain features. They must be appropriate for their purpose and aligned with quality learning goals to enable teachers to make inferences about student progress toward the learning goal. Quality tools are valid and reliable, which means that the tools measure what they are intended to measure and do so consistently and reliably. For more information on measuring validity and reliability, see the "Classroom Assessment—General" section in Resource A.

Quality tools must elicit the full range of student understanding of the content as appropriate for the grade level. The tool must also be accurate in measuring student understanding. Accuracy is more likely when quality criteria address clear expectations for teachers and students and when the quality tools are fair and unbiased. The tasks should enable students of different genders, ethnicities, and language groups to understand what is being assessed and to perform well. The criteria should guide teachers toward an unbiased interpretation of student responses. A final feature for quality tools is one of practicality because time for teaching and learning is limited in all classrooms. Assessments need to be efficient and feasible to ensure that teachers have time to analyze student responses and use the information to improve student learning.

Quality Use

Quality use is how teachers interpret and use the evidence about student understanding that they collect with quality tools. The strategic use of quality tools to support student learning is integral to the pedagogical practice of Assessment-Centered Teaching. Evidence from quality assessment tools can be used to guide instruction, provide feedback to students, involve students in accountability and reflection, and refine instructional materials and critique and revise assessments for future implementation.

Of course, the quality of the use of the data depends on the sound interpretation of that data. Assessment-centered teachers understand that, in addition to paying attention to the knowledge represented by the vertices of the assessment knowledge triangle, one must also pay close attention to the lines or relationships between these points. This brings us to a discussion of Figure 2.3, which explains these relationships.

Figure 2.3   *ACT Framework* Expanded Assessment Knowledge Triangle: Focus on Lines

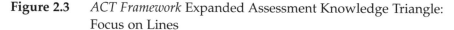

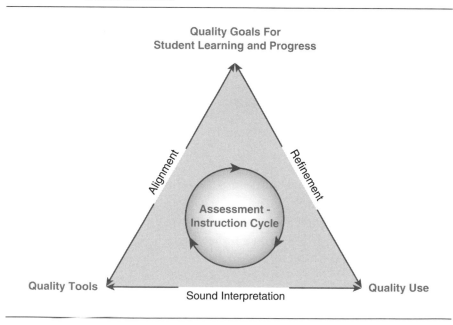

In Figure 2.3, the vertices are gray-scaled, focusing attention on the relationships between the vertices: *Sound Interpretation* as a relationship between Quality Tools and Quality Use, *Alignment* as a relationship between Quality Tools and Quality Goals for Student Learning and Progress, and *Refinement* as a relationship between Quality Use and Quality Goals for Student Learning and Progress.

Sound Interpretation

The interplay between the vertices of the triangle is so intertwined that describing the lines may seem redundant. However, this redundancy can be helpful in strengthening teachers' assessment knowledge and practice. For example, an interpretation can be sound only if it is aligned with the initial learning goals and based on information collected with a quality tool. When teachers interpret student work, they reflect on issues that require they pay attention to many elements of the *ACT Framework:* Are my criteria aligned with my learning goals? Do they capture the full range of student understanding of targeted learning goals? Have I scored consistently? To what extent does my analysis of class performance reflect the opportunities of all my students to learn the curriculum? (Gearhart et al., 2006).

Alignment

Alignment represents the relationship between Quality Goals for Student Learning and Progress and Quality Tools, yet it is also a key component of Sound Interpretation. When teachers interpret student work, they reflect on how the tool relates to learning goals: Does the tool in fact measure the learning goal? At what level does the tool measure the content understanding? Is the tool fair and unbiased? Does it provide opportunities to capture a range of student understanding? Are expectations clear for students? Is the tool efficient and feasible for the scope of the content to be assessed?

Refinement

Refinement describes the variety of ways in which evidence from sound interpretations of student work can be used: to monitor and adjust instruction, refine instructional materials, and refine assessments. When teachers adjust or refine their instruction, they reflect on the sequence of learning: What gaps in student learning are evident in student work? What instructional revisions might be needed to close these gaps? What additional or supplemental activities should be added to the learning sequence to help students progress toward a learning goal? When teachers refine assessments, they reflect on the quality of the tool: How does the task structure enable students to respond? What needs to be refined in the task and/or the criteria to better elicit student understanding on their progress toward the learning goals?

ACT Framework Expanded: Assessment-Instruction Cycle

The second component of the *Assessment-Centered Teaching Framework* is the Assessment-Instruction Cycle in the center of the triangle in Figure 2.1 and expanded in Figure 2.4.

This cycle depicts quality assessment practice—the ways that assessment-centered teachers plan, implement, and use evidence

Figure 2.4   Assessment-Instruction Cycle

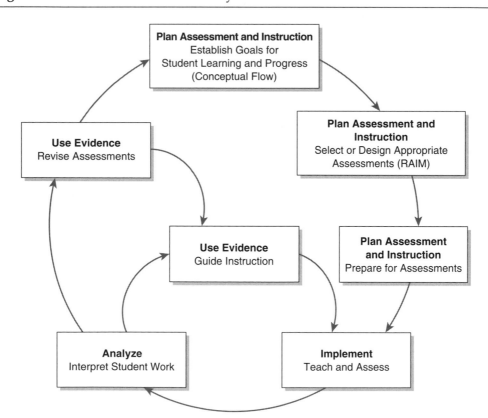

to reflect on their practices and the impact of their practices on student achievement.

The cycle begins when teachers determine their Quality Goals for Student Learning and Progress. Assessment-centered teachers reflect on what should be taught, focusing on the big ideas or concepts of the discipline, standards, and curriculum. Teachers develop a Conceptual Flow (DiRanna, 1989; DiRanna & Topps, 2004) of the concepts students should know and understand about a certain topic. The Conceptual Flow process allows teachers to unpack and organize the content their students will need to know to achieve understanding of the big ideas of science. (See Chapter 4 for a discussion of Conceptual Flow.) These carefully selected concepts ultimately become the learning goals for the unit of instruction, are organized for an instructional sequence, and serve as the targeted goals for the assessment plan.

The next step in the cycle is to construct an assessment plan. Using a process we termed the Record of Assessment in Instructional Materials (RAIM), assessment-centered teachers identify appropriate assessment points in their instructional Conceptual Flow and then select potentially appropriate assessment tools in their instructional materials to measure student learning. (See Chapter 5 for a discussion of RAIM.) These key assessment points—usually a pre-assessment, a post-assessment, and a series of critical juncture assessments—monitor student progress toward the learning goals. For each targeted goal, the assessments answer key questions:

- What does each student know before the unit begins (pre-assessment)?
- What does the student understand about the concept at critical points in the unit (juncture assessments)?
- What does the student understand about the concept at the end of the unit (post-assessment)?

The last step in planning is to prepare for the assessments. In this step, teachers reflect on their assessment plan and determine how best to instruct students so that they can demonstrate their understanding via the assessments. Teachers reflect on the assessment tasks and determine how they will administer the tasks. Lastly, teachers select target students to monitor student progress in a strategic manner.

Once planning is complete, teachers implement the unit of instruction, integrating the assessments as they teach. When teachers interpret the student work, they score and analyze the responses for whole class patterns and trends in student understanding. Based on the analysis of student work, the assessment-centered teacher considers the implications for instruction for individuals and groups. In addition, analysis from student work may reveal the quality of the assessment tools and the role they played in providing evidence of student understanding. A teacher may decide that a weak tool has provided weak evidence and implement a different assessment to provide better information. Or the teacher may decide to revise the assessment for future implementation of the same unit. The Assessment-Instruction Cycle begins anew with the next unit of study.

Moving Toward Reflective Practice

The *Assessment-Centered Teaching Framework* is the theoretical basis of the Science Assessment Leadership Academy. To actualize this foundational knowledge and practice, we designed a professional development strategy based on principles of effective and transformative teacher learning (Loucks-Horsley, Love, Stiles, Mundry, & Hewson, 2003; Thompson & Zeuli, 1999). Our strategy emphasized reflective practice through the *Assessment-Centered Teaching Portfolio*. The strategy enabled us to create a learning community of teachers working to strengthen their expertise with assessment, and more. Our community also provided ample opportunity for teachers to reflect on and examine and challenge current practice to bring about fundamental change in assumptions and beliefs about teaching and learning. In Chapter 3, we provide an overview of our program strategy, and in Chapters 4–10, we share the tools and processes of this strategy.

3

Reflective Practice

The *Assessment-Centered Teaching (ACT) Portfolio*

In this chapter, we discuss the importance of reflective practice to change and enhance teaching. We introduce our reflective practice strategy, the *Assessment-Centered Teaching (ACT) Portfolio,* to acquaint the reader with the rationale for the strategy. Chapters 4–12 will provide a detailed description of the portfolio as well as information from our research on the impact of its use.

Reflective Practice

A classroom that is thriving is an environment of complex interactions. Teachers engage students with conceptual content, scaffold learning by monitoring student understanding through classroom assessment (NRC, 2001), and refine instructional approaches based on evidence. At every moment in the classroom, teachers make hundreds of instructional decisions—some instinctively, some based on planning, and some "just because." We wanted teachers to make *intentional* decisions as reflective practitioners.

Assessment-centered teachers become "researchers in the context of practice" (Schön, 1983, p. 68) by reflecting on learning goals and taking informed action based on feedback from student products.

These teachers mine student thinking to determine their current schema and design ways to connect new learning to what students already know (Bransford, Brown, & Cocking, 1999). Assessment-centered teachers reflect on their students' understanding through analysis of classroom interactions as well as paper-pencil assessments. By triangulating evidence from several sources, teachers determine how fragile or firm student understanding is at any point in the learning cycle and adjust instruction accordingly. These teachers truly engage in "reflection-on-action" (Schön).

We recognized that this type of reflection was not the norm in most classrooms and that if we wanted to bring about Assessment-Centered Teaching, we needed to provide professional development experiences that would help teachers see the power of assessment for learning (Stiggins, 2002) and redefine teaching as the integration of assessment and instruction. The *ACT Portfolio* provided these kinds of experiences.

The *ACT Portfolio*

A centerpiece of the ACT process is the *ACT Portfolio,* a reflective tool that supports teachers as they develop and use assessments for each curriculum unit, and documents their growth in Assessment-Centered Teaching. Portfolios are a fairly common professional tool that support teacher learning and have been found to scaffold teacher reflection and encourage improvements in practice (Edgerton, Hutchings, & Quinlan, 1991; Shulman, 1998). While most teacher portfolios focus on instructional improvement, ours focused primarily on assessment. Our intent was not to use the *ACT Portfolio* for evaluation of teachers' assessment practices but instead as a "learning portfolio" (Wolf & Dietz, 1998) and a means of continuous improvement. The *ACT Portfolio* provided reflective scaffolds for teachers' thinking and examples to guide teachers with Assessment-Centered Teaching. The completed portfolios became archives for teachers to review and to share with colleagues, and they also served as evidence for our research on the ways that teachers build expertise with Assessment-Centered Teaching. Because it was a portable tool that could travel to and from the classroom and Academy meetings, the *ACT Portfolio* enabled teachers to reflect individually as well as collaboratively and encouraged their reflections both orally and in writing.

The *ACT Portfolio* and our supporting professional development activities proved effective strategies for promoting teacher reflection and developing strong habits for purposeful instruction. As one teacher stated:

> *Defining and clarifying instructional goals before class became routine. Basing real-time instructional decisions on students' responses also became the norm in my classroom. Sharing expectations with my students seemed to motivate them because they knew what I expected. Analyses of my students' work forced me to think deeply about individual performances and the effectiveness of my teaching.*

Use of the *ACT Portfolio* allowed us to document teacher change, the focus of our work. As noted above, the *ACT Portfolio* was a major impetus for creating teacher change. Additionally, although student change was not an explicit focus of our work, teachers reported effective changes in student understanding and achievement. Carrie Green, a middle school teacher, worked closely with her school's science department over her three-year participation in CAESL. She engaged the department in reflective practice, using the *ACT Portfolio*, and guided the department to develop an assessment-centered instruction plan. During the third year of implementation, they observed a significant schoolwide increase in student achievement as evidenced by scores on standardized tests for science. Yvette, our teacher from Chapter 1, reported measurable classroom gains as a result of obtaining evidence about student learning through reflective assessment practices. She noted that this evidence led to changes in her instructional practice of targeted support for individual students.

The *ACT Portfolio* is aligned with the Assessment-Instruction Cycle (discussed in Chapter 2 and included here as Figure 3.1). It is divided into phases based on what the teacher is actively doing in practice and in reflection.

Table 3.1 orients the reader to the phases in the cycle, the corresponding phases of the *ACT Portfolio* that guide teacher reflection, and the chapter in the book in which each *ACT Portfolio* phase and process is explained in more detail. The actual portfolio forms can be found on the enclosed CD-ROM.

Figure 3.1   Portfolio Template Aligned with Assessment-Instruction Cycle

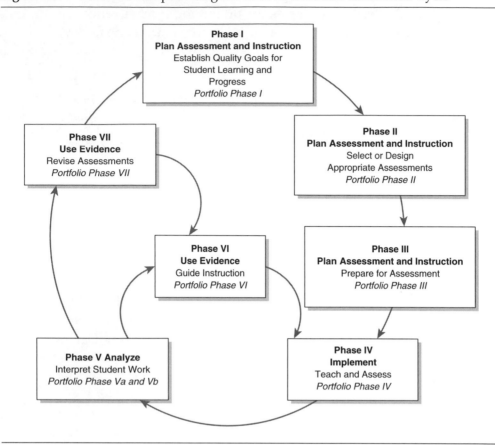

Table 3.1   *ACT Portfolio* Aligned With Chapters*

Phase in Assessment-Instruction Cycle	ACT Portfolio *Phases:*	*Chapter*
Phase I Plan Assessment and Instruction: Establish Quality Goals for Student Learning and Progress	*Phase I: Conceptual Flow* • Individual Pre-think • Collaborative Pre-think • Match to Instructional Materials • Align to Standards • Review Progression of Flow	Chapter 4
Phase II Plan Assessment and Instruction: Select or Design Appropriate Assessments	*Phase II: Record of Assessments in Instructional Materials* • Pre-think Assessment Points • Match Assessments to Assessment Points • Select Assessment Plan (pre-, post-, and juncture assessments) • Develop Expected Student Responses for Selected Assessments • Reflection on Coherence Between Conceptual Flow and Assessment Plan	Chapter 5
Phase III Plan Assessment and Instruction: Prepare for Assessment	*Phase III: Prepare for Assessments* • Prepare for Instruction • Communicate Performance Expectations and Plan Feedback • Administer Assessment • Select Target Students	Chapter 6
Phase IV Implement: Teach and Assess	*Phase IV: Reflection*	
Phase V Analyze: Interpret Student Work	*Phase Va: Develop Criteria* • Review Expected Student Responses • Sort Student Responses • Develop Criteria • Score Student Responses	Chapter 7
Phase V Analyze: Interpret Student Work	*Phase Vb: Analyze Patterns and Trends* • Identify Type of Information Needed From Assessment • Identify Appropriate Units Analysis • Identify Appropriate Items Analysis • Select Type of Assessment Record • Ask Questions of the Data	Chapter 8
Phase VI Use Evidence: Guide Instruction	*Phase VI* • Identify General Patterns and Possible Interventions • Identify Specific Revisions in Instruction • Plan Feedback to Students	Chapter 9
Phase VII Use Evidence: Revise Assessments	*Phase VII* • Match Assessment Tools to the Learning Goals • Evaluate the Quality of the Tool • Revise the Assessment Tool • Administer Revised Assessment and Collect Data	Chapter 10

*All *ACT Portfolio* forms are found in Resource B on the CD-ROM.

The Importance of Reflective Practice

Bass and Glaser (2004) argue that reflective dialogues among teachers should be the basis for classrooms of the future where there is comparative reflection between the teacher and students. In the future, classrooms will provide

> an environment of interchange interspersed by periods of reflection and problem solving. The teachers' reflection comes about as a result of interpretation of student performance; the students' reflection is the result of their reactions to feedback presented over the course of learning. There are periods in which both teachers and students appear to come together in appreciation that their activity has been successful, with the teachers planning next steps and the students anticipating the development of new knowledge. (p. 20)

Our approach has shown that this type of classroom is possible. Teachers who use reflective practice can build assessment-centered classrooms today.

Chapters 4 through 10 address how this happens through the *ACT Portfolio* process. As we discuss the phases and the processes we used to facilitate them, we consider their

- relationships to the *Assessment-Centered Teaching Framework,*
- purposes,
- roles in building reflective practice, and
- impact on teacher learning.

These four elements provide the basic structure for each chapter. Additionally, each chapter includes examples from teachers' *ACT Portfolios* that show how teachers used them to reflect on their work. These examples are not exemplars; rather, they serve to illustrate how teachers can build their skills as assessment-centered teachers.

4

Plan Assessment and Instruction

ACT Portfolio
Phase I
Steps
1, 2, 3, 4

Establish Quality Goals for Student Learning and Progress by Developing the Conceptual Flow

In this chapter, we discuss Phase I of the Assessment-Instruction Cycle, where the assessment-centered teacher plans for assessment and instruction. This chapter describes the Conceptual Flow as a tool and process that helps teachers establish quality student learning goals and eventually establish the framework for their assessment plan. We provide two examples of teacher work, one elementary and one secondary, illustrating teachers' thinking in developing a Conceptual Flow.

"Conceptual Flow" and the *Assessment-Centered Teaching Framework*

The development of the Conceptual Flow is Phase I of the *Assessment-Instruction Cycle* (Figure 2.4) for any

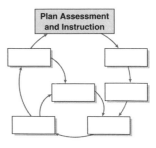

new unit of instruction. In this phase, assessment-centered teachers begin to think about the content they want students to know and understand. Using the Conceptual Flow process in the *ACT Portfolio*, teachers identify concepts that eventually serve as the Quality Goals for Student Learning and Progress vertex of the Assessment Knowledge Triangle (Figure 2.2). Once established, the Conceptual Flow serves as the basis for the assessment plan.

Purpose of "Conceptual Flow"

The Conceptual Flow is a determination of where you are going in your teaching and what you're going to reflect on. You have to know what concepts are important and the order in which they go to conceptualize the whole learning. I put my conceptual flow on the wall for the kids so they learn where they're going, too.

—Academy Teacher

Starting with the end in mind and backward planning (Wiggins & McTighe, 2005) have been heralded as means for setting comprehensible goals and designing better instruction. The Conceptual Flow is a backward-planning tool. Teachers array the big ideas that are important for students to know, the standards they are responsible for teaching, and the content presented in the instructional materials into one comprehensive, sequential chart. As teachers identify and integrate these three elements, the process of constructing a Conceptual Flow enables teachers to clearly identify specific Quality Goals for Student Learning and Progress.

Developed in 1989 by the K–12 Alliance/WestEd, the Conceptual Flow process is grounded in the practical work of teachers and supported by research on learning. Creating a Conceptual Flow assists teachers in developing learning goals that align with the National Research Council's synthesis of cognitive research, *How People Learn: Bridging Research and Practice* (Donovan, Bransford, & Pellegrino, 1999), which states that to develop competence in an area of inquiry, students must

a. have a deep foundation of factual knowledge,
b. understand facts and ideas in the context of a conceptual framework, and
c. organize knowledge in ways that facilitate retrieval and application. (p. 12)

The Conceptual Flow also assists students by making them aware of the links in the concepts they are addressing. Too often, it is a mystery to students why they are learning what they are learning. When a Conceptual Flow is displayed in the classroom, it allows both teachers and students to connect new ideas and information, providing opportunities to learn with deeper understanding.

> When asked what they teach, many teachers answer with a topic; when asked what students should know about that topic, many teachers provide a list of facts. Developing Conceptual Flows helps teachers build foundational knowledge about the importance of helping students to construct conceptual frameworks rather than "learn" factual information.

Thus, the completed Conceptual Flow serves the following four purposes:

1. Details the important concepts and linkages to other ideas;

2. Identifies an instructional sequence for which resources (e.g., textbooks, instructional materials) can be used to support teaching;

3. Identifies important concepts for assessment of student understanding;

4. Eventually serves as the foundation of an assessment plan for the unit of instruction.

The Conceptual Flow is both a product *and* a process. As a product, it resembles a map of nested concepts (Figure 4.1). The biggest ideas are supported by small ideas, and those small ideas are maintained by even smaller ideas, which become learning sequence concepts. The lines that connect ideas are drawn in different widths to indicate the strength of the links between concepts. For example, thicker lines indicate a strong link, while thinner lines indicate a weaker link. The Conceptual Flow differs from a concept map in that it addresses concepts in a unit of instruction and has both a hierarchy of ideas (indicating the relationships between and among the ideas) and a direction (i.e., the sequence for instruction of the unit).

> The Conceptual Flow is an instructional sequence of concepts and supporting ideas nested in a hierarchy. The links between and among concepts and supporting concepts are explicit as are the relationships of learning sequence concepts to supporting concepts and bigger ideas (concepts).

In sum, as a process, constructing the Conceptual Flow is a springboard for teachers' conversations about teaching and learning

Figure 4.1   Building (Identifying) the Conceptual Flow

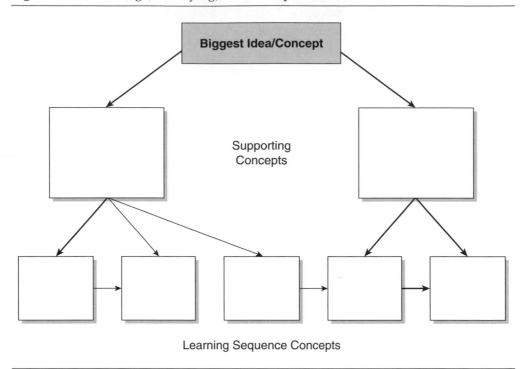

as well as an opportunity to strengthen their content knowledge. The resulting product can be shared with students to make public what teachers want students to know and understand.

Role of "Conceptual Flow" in Building Reflective Practice

An individual teacher can develop a Conceptual Flow, but the quality of the flow and the opportunities for teacher learning are greatly enriched when teachers work collaboratively. Often teachers work in grade-level and/or content-related teams to construct a Conceptual Flow with the support of a facilitator who has content and pedagogical content knowledge, knowledge of instructional materials and standards, and facilitation skills. The reflective, analytical, and iterative nature of the Conceptual Flow process "deprivatizes" practice among team members (Louis, Kruse, & Bryk, 1995) and enables the team to define what conceptual understanding of the content should look like for a unit of instruction.

The process of building the Conceptual Flow for a unit of instruction includes these five steps:

---

1. Conduct an individual pre-think of the important concepts students should understand about a big idea.

2. Create with the team a collaborative pre-think from the individual pre-thinks.

3. Match the collaborative pre-think to concepts in the instructional materials.

4. Align concepts from the collaborative pre-think and instructional materials to content standards.

5. Review the progression of concepts and place them in an instructional sequence that provides strong links for student understanding.

A more detailed description of each of the steps follows. Figures 4.3a–d reveal the development of a Conceptual Flow for an elementary unit of instruction, *Earth Materials* (Full Option Science System [FOSS], 2001); Figures 4.4a–d reveal the development of a Conceptual Flow for a secondary genetics unit of instruction from *Biology: A Human Approach* (Biological Sciences Curriculum Studies [BSCS], 2003).

1. Conduct an Individual Pre-think of the Important Concepts Students Should Understand About a Big Idea

Teachers are given the following prompt: "What should an exiting ___ grader understand about [content for an instructional unit]?" For example, sixth-grade teachers might be prompted to respond to the following: "What should an exiting sixth grader understand about weather?" The expectation is that teachers respond independently in writing, answering with complete sentences in a paragraph format. Asking teachers to construct complete sentences results in more concept-like statements rather than one-word topics and challenges teachers to think more deeply about what understanding might look like for their students.

> Teachers often begin a Conceptual Flow by offering vocabulary (e.g., *convection*) for concepts. The use of probing questions (e.g., How does convection play a role in weather systems?) helps teachers identify what is really important for their students to know and understand. Teachers also confront their depth of content knowledge and discover when they need to seek other resources.

Teachers then use their understanding of facts and concepts to determine the "grain size" of the ideas they have written. They determine which ideas are supported by one another, nesting smaller ideas to support bigger ideas. They also determine which concepts connect or provide links to other concepts. Asking teachers to write their concepts and facts on different-sized sticky notes (one per note) helps them with this nesting/linking activity.

> Teachers often need experience nesting and linking concepts, subconcepts, and facts. Discussions with colleagues help teachers construct how both facts and concepts fit into an instructional sequence. To develop common definitions and language among our teachers, throughout the Conceptual Flow process, we spent time discussing whether particular ideas were at the definitional level (a fact: insects have six legs and three body parts) or represented a more complex relationship (a concept: how the structures of living things are related to particular functions).

One might wonder about the rationale for starting with a pre-think rather than beginning with examining the standards or the instructional materials. The answer is quite simple. The process mirrors what we know from research (e.g., *How People Learn,* Bransford, Brown, & Cocking, 1999) about the importance of accessing learners' prior knowledge. By asking for teachers' thinking up front, we acknowledge teachers' professionalism and provide an opportunity for teachers to reflect on their prior ideas about the important and appropriate content for their students. By accessing their related prior knowledge, teachers also create a rich intellectual and linguistic context that helps them to understand more deeply the strengths and weaknesses of the conceptual development provided in their materials or standards. Once teachers examine their thinking about particular concepts, they can more readily align and reconcile their "conceptual story" with that found in the materials.

2. Create With the Team a Collaborative Pre-think From the Individual Pre-thinks

The next step is for colleagues to share their written ideas with the rest of the group. As they explain their thinking, they post each concept on a large sheet of chart paper where the entire group can see it (Figure 4.2). Through professional discourse and reflection, the team identifies where there is overlap in their thinking and acknowledges concepts they may not have individually considered. As the group continues to process the concepts, they move and combine each other's sticky notes so that bigger ideas and concepts are placed with smaller ideas nested below. Through this process, a concept might be upgraded to a larger idea; this is noted in Figure 4.2 where a small

Figure 4.2 Collaborative Pre-think: Preliminary Conceptual Flow

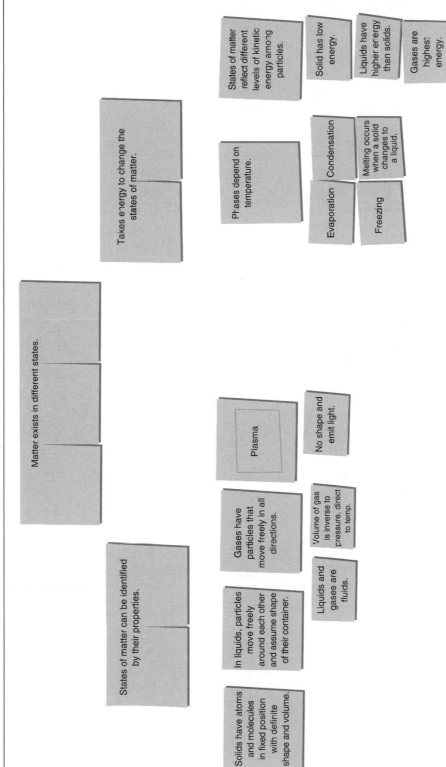

sticky note has been placed on a larger sticky note. Through continued reflection, the team agrees on a preliminary Conceptual Flow for the unit of instruction. This is represented in Figure 4.2 by the arrangement of the sticky notes from left to right.

Once the preliminary Conceptual Flow is posted in front of the group, the quality of the flow can be enhanced by further reflection using these questions:

- Are the major concepts of the topic addressed in the flow?
- Are the concepts in the flow developmentally appropriate?
- Is the flow (i.e., the sequence of concepts) developmentally appropriate?
- How are the smaller concepts/ideas nested so as to support the bigger ideas?
- How are concepts linked in ways that help to build understanding?

The sticky note Conceptual Flow represents the teachers' current thinking about content for a unit of instruction. It is now time to match this flow with the flow of concepts in the instructional materials.

3. Match the Collaborative Pre-think to Concepts in the Instructional Materials

The dual purposes of identifying the Conceptual Flow in the instructional materials are (1) to understand how the developers of the instructional materials thought about the conceptual development in the unit and (2) to compare the unit flow with the teachers' ideas about how conceptual understanding is built. Through the Conceptual Flow process, the instructional materials become more transparent to teachers. The goals are to craft the most appropriate instructional sequence for students and to ensure that teachers have deep understanding of that sequence.

To identify the concepts in the instructional materials, teachers (or teams) read the entire unit/chapter/module that addresses the major concepts they wish to teach. Teachers record all the concepts they find in the instructional materials, then create a flow of the concepts according to their presentation in the instructional materials. Using differently sized arrows, teachers can indicate the strength of the connections of the concepts addressed in the instructional materials.

Figure 4.3a illustrates one team's interpretation of the Conceptual Flow found in the Grades 3–4 *Earth Materials* (FOSS, 2001) instructional materials. It represents what teachers thought are the important concepts of the unit and the order in which they are presented. The size of arrows (or their absence) indicates where the teachers thought there are links in the instructional materials. Figure 4.4a illustrates the Conceptual Flow on genetics created by a high school biology team working with *Biology: A Human Approach* (BSCS, 2003). Like the elementary school example, this secondary Conceptual Flow also represents the teachers' interpretation of the important concepts from the instructional materials and the order in which they are developed during instruction.

> It is important to note that teachers' Conceptual Flows may or may not match the curriculum developer's intent. These flows represent the sense making on the part of the teachers that will help them determine appropriate and quality goals for student learning.

Once the Conceptual Flow of the instructional materials is identified, teachers compare it to their collaborative pre-think for the unit. This comparison leads to several possible insights, including the following:

- Teachers may discover that ideas they thought important were left out of the instructional materials.
- They may find extraneous ideas in the instructional materials that are not important for conceptual understanding.
- They may find new ideas in the materials that are important to teach for conceptual understanding.

The teachers must then decide how to reconcile the concepts from both the pre-think and the instructional materials into a single Conceptual Flow for the whole unit. By arranging the concepts into an instructional sequence, the teachers are developing a plan for the flow of learning.

Figures 4.3b and 4.4b represent the elementary team's amalgam of their pre-think and the concepts found in the *Earth Materials* (FOSS, 2001) unit. The team identified a good match with the exception of three concepts in their pre-think. They decided that two of these concepts (rocks form, erode, and re-form through the rock cycle; and rock and mineral products can be used by humans) could be addressed in another unit, but the remaining concept (objects can be observed) was crucial to building student understanding in this unit. The teachers recognized that a strong focus on literacy had provided little science experience in the primary grades, resulting in little knowledge of basic science processes. They decided to include this concept in their amalgam Conceptual Flow. Shadowed boxes in Figure 4.3b represent this concept and its supporting concepts.

The secondary school team also found a good match between their pre-think and the instructional material's Conceptual Flow. One notable exception became apparent as the teachers discussed the instructional sequence. Considering the background of their students (many English-Language Learners) and their lack of science experience (the middle school science program was focused on literacy), the teachers thought that quality learning goals needed to include an introductory scaffold. On the Conceptual Flow displayed in Figure 4.4b, this scaffold is represented by the first concept, "Like begets like." The team used their pedagogical content knowledge to identify appropriate supporting concepts (noted in the shadowed boxes) and to reflect at length about how they would create a bridge from these supporting concepts to the first larger concept in the unit. The larger arrows represent what they thought were the strongest connections between concepts.

4. Align Concepts From the Collaborative Pre-think and Instructional Materials to Content Standards

Since the adoption of national and state content standards, educators have been aligning their curriculum and instruction with these documents to improve student understanding. In the Academy, teachers' discussions about alignment between standards and the Conceptual Flow inevitably raised challenging issues about the meaning of content in the standards. We think of this process as "unpacking" the standards to identify better the knowledge and skills that they represent. Unpacking the standards helps teachers become more grounded in what is important to teach and why, enriches their understanding of the content, and helps enormously as they plan for instruction and assessment.

> The dialogue and decision making that accompany the process of building a Conceptual Flow aligns with the challenge set forth by Wolf (1994): "We need standards that remain alive to the ongoing conversation about what knowledge is. . . . Without that the standards will freeze in place" (p. 88).

The alignment of standards to the Conceptual Flow involves matching the standard (and its intent) with the preliminary Conceptual Flow from Step 3 (the amalgam of the pre-think and the instructional materials). Figure 4.3c represents a standards match between the elementary school Conceptual Flow and standards documents, and Figure 4.4c represents a standards match between the high school Conceptual Flow and standards documents.

The following documents are cited on these figures with these abbreviations:

- *National Science Education Standards* (National Research Council [NRC], 1996) for "Earth Science Content Standards Grades K–4" and for "Life Science Content Standards Grades 9–12." Abbreviation: NSES
- *Benchmarks for Scientific Literacy* (American Association for the Advancement of Science [AAAS], 1993). Abbreviation: BMKS
- *California Science Content Standards* (California Department of Education, 2000). Abbreviation: CA

Notice in both figures that some concepts are supported by all of the standards documents, while others may be supported by one, two, or none of the documents. Variations in alignment may be due to the differences in the depth of the standards or to teachers' views that concepts not covered in the standards are nevertheless important in the unit.

Aligning the Conceptual Flow with standards may include refining concepts, adding or deleting concepts at a grade level to be more reflective of the standards, moving concepts to another grade level, or none of the above if the team feels that standards are met by the current Conceptual Flow. In Figures 4.3d and 4.4d, the non-aligned concepts are considered by the teachers to be important parts of student understanding and are left in the Conceptual Flow for that reason.

5. Review the Progression of Concepts and Place Them in an Instructional Sequence That Provides Strong Links for Student Understanding

The Conceptual Flow now represents a composite of the teachers' thinking, the concepts in the instructional materials, and the content addressed in the standards. Teachers now review the overall instructional relevance of the sequence of the flow by asking the following questions: Are the concepts nested and linked to help build student understanding? Is the flow (i.e., the sequence of concepts) developmentally appropriate? Does the arrangement of concepts anticipate alternative conceptions students might have as part of their prior knowledge? Are concepts that are not aligned to standards essential for the students' conceptual understanding?

In this final arrangement phase, individual teachers construct a graphic organizer of their Conceptual Flow to use in their classrooms. The format of the graphic organizer is the teacher's choice and often reflects a teacher's personal preferences and needs at a given grade level. Many teachers prefer to use a Conceptual Flow with boxes and arrows as noted in the prior figures. Other teachers choose a graphic organizer that will work well posted on a bulletin board. Figures 4.3d and 4.4d provide examples of these graphic organizers. No matter the format, the graphic should clearly depict the concepts and their relationships to each other, enabling teachers and students to see which concepts are big ideas, which are supporting ideas, and how ideas are linked. The graphic organizer, posted in the classroom, is a visual reminder of what the students are learning and where they are headed in terms of the learning goals.

The following graphics represent the work of elementary school teachers (Figures 4.3a-4.3d) and high school teachers (Figures 4.4a-4.4d) as they used the Conceptual Flow to develop learning goals for their students.

- Figure 4.3a shows the concepts from the instructional materials.
- Figure 4.3b is an amalgam of the teachers' original pre-think and their interpretation of the instructional materials.
- Figure 4.3c is a standards match between the Conceptual Flow and standards documents.
- Figure 4.3d represents a graphic organizer of the Conceptual Flow.
- Figure 4.4a represents the concepts from the instructional materials.
- Figure 4.4b is an amalgam of the teachers' original pre-think and their interpretation of the instructional materials.
- Figure 4.4c is a standards match between the Conceptual Flow and standards documents.
- Figure 4.4d is a graphic organizer of the Conceptual Flow.

After completing the Conceptual Flow, assessment-centered teachers have identified an appropriate instructional sequence for their students based on deep reflection about the teaching and learning of specific concepts. Teachers come to understand that the Conceptual Flow represents a dynamic and intricate relationship among content, instructional materials, standards, and assessment. It

(Text continues on Page 57)

Figure 4.3a   Teacher Interpretation of the Conceptual Flow in Instructional Materials FOSS *Earth Materials* Grades 3–4

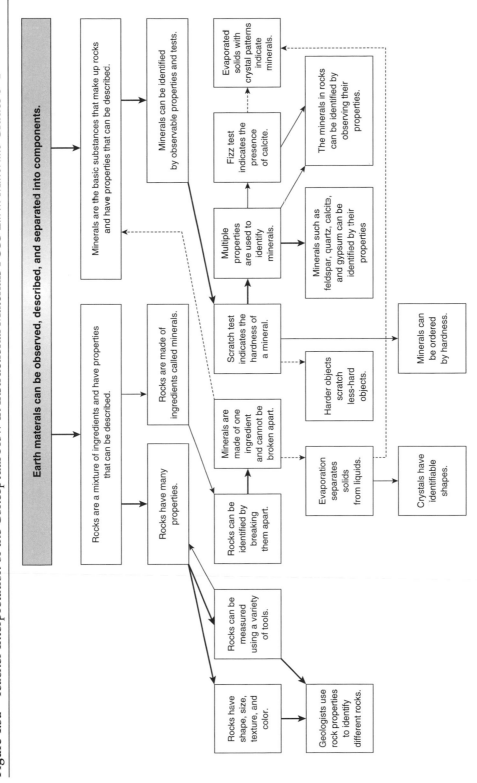

Figure 4.3b Pre-think and Instructional Materials Amalgam

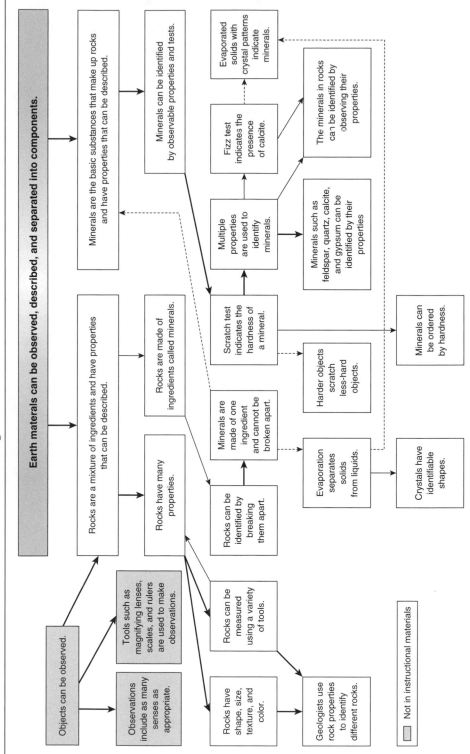

Figure 4.3c Conceptual Flow Aligned to Standards

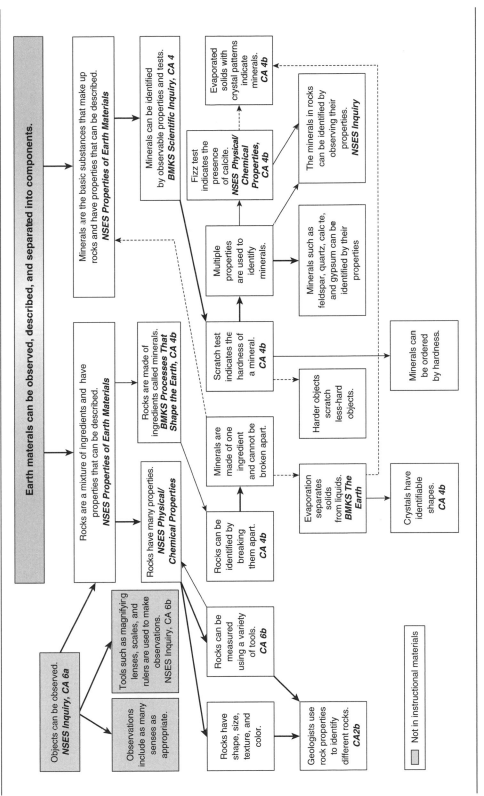

52

Figure 4.3d Graphic Organizer for Conceptual Flow

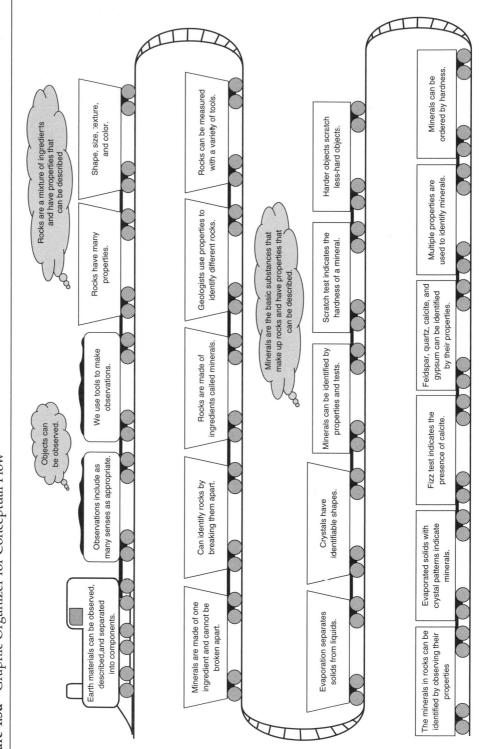

Figure 4.4a Teacher Interpretation of the Conceptual Flow in Instructional Materials BSCS *Biology: A Human Approach* Genetics

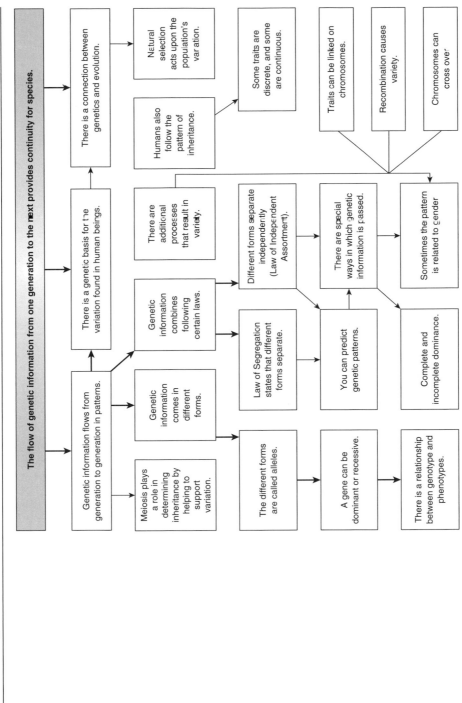

Figure 4.4b Pre-think and Instructional Materials Amalgam

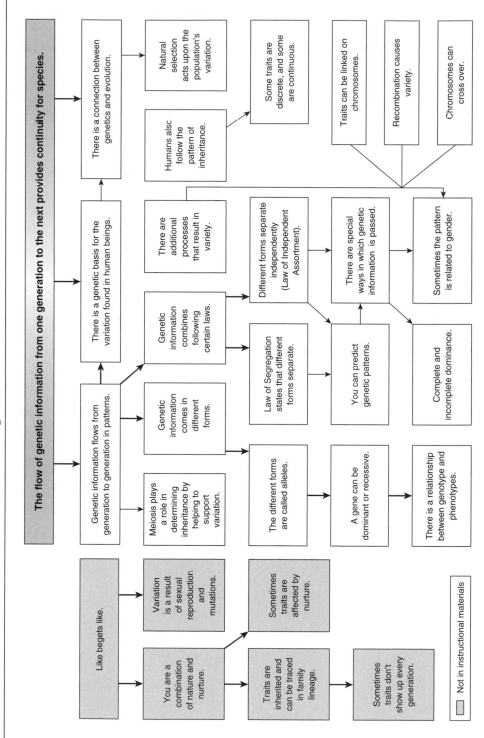

Figure 4.4c Conceptual Flow Aligned to Standards

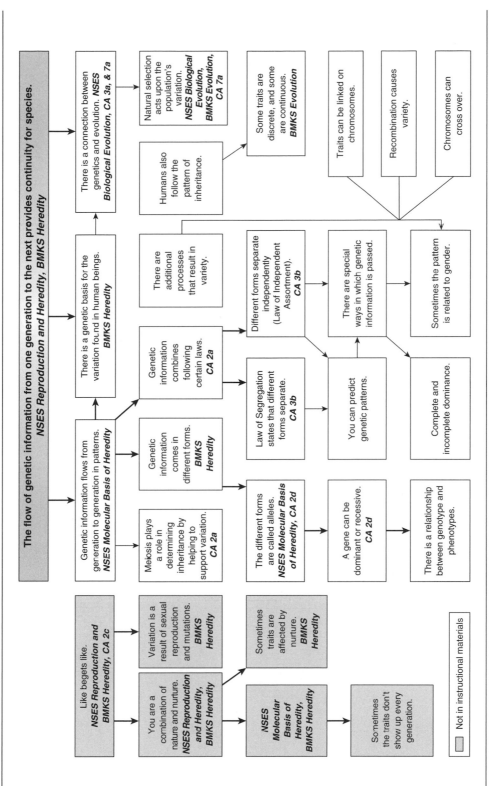

Figure 4.4d Graphic Organizer for Conceptual Flow

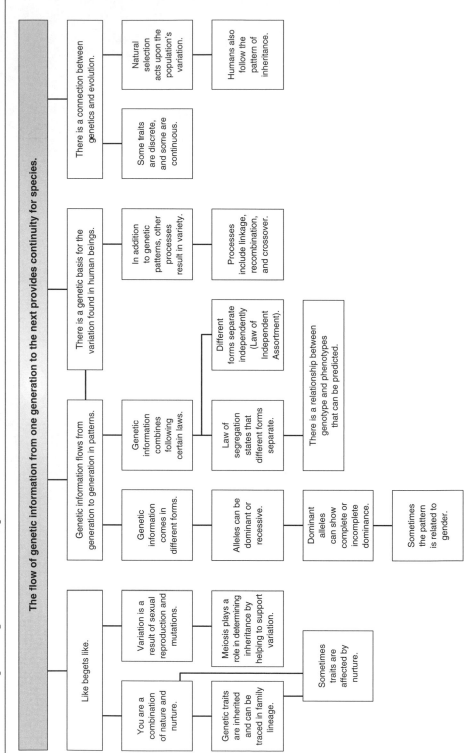

The flow of genetic information from one generation to the next provides continuity for species.

is important to emphasize that Conceptual Flows are fluid and open to revision as assessment-centered teachers continue in the Assessment-Instruction Cycle, teaching the unit, interpreting student work, and using assessment data to refine their instruction, materials, and assessments.

Quality Conceptual Flows are not simple to construct. Teachers must think differently about the content they teach and reach consensus on challenging issues. With practice, teachers become more facile at developing Conceptual Flows. But even with experience, the Conceptual Flow should never be considered finished. Assessment-centered teachers deepen their understanding of content and pedagogical content knowledge as they revisit and revise their flow, recognizing where students truly made links and where gaps in instruction may have left students unable to make connections between concepts.

"Conceptual Flow" and Teacher Change

Throughout the Academy, researchers interviewed and surveyed teachers about the effects of the Academy program and *ACT Portfolio* on their classroom practice. When asked to identify the Academy tool or process that impacted them the most, many teachers cited the Conceptual Flow as a highly useful way to develop their plan for instruction and assessment. For example:

> *I think teachers need to understand the conceptual flow of their curriculum . . . what concepts they want students to learn; what concepts to assess with their students. . . . Then they can plan for teaching.*

> *[Developing the Conceptual Flow] moved us from a list of topics to . . . nesting of important ideas. Identifying what really matters for student understanding drives decisions about . . . questions in the assessment.*

In a political climate that stresses coverage of material in preparation for state testing, teachers appreciate that building Conceptual Flows provides them with a process to think beyond the standards checklists and pacing guides and focus on conceptual understanding. One teacher explained,

My district is into curriculum mapping and . . . I'm trying to cover the standards, but [by using the Conceptual Flow] you have to go deeper into the standards to assess the concepts that are actually behind the understanding, instead of just checking off standards.

Based on the researchers' findings, the benefits of the Conceptual Flow appear to go beyond assessment planning: teachers *take ownership of* their instruction by becoming better consumers of instructional materials. As they grapple with important concepts and how they should be arranged in a meaningful sequence, teachers gain insight into how instructional materials are organized; which materials are designed to support student understanding of the big ideas; and which lessons, resources, and assessments need to be revised. Teachers can then modify their instruction and assessment practice to address any gaps or weaknesses. Academy teachers commented:

With a new focus on the concepts in the conceptual flow, I was able to really see my instructional materials. I mean, I knew that our instructional materials were not often perfect, but this really brought out where the holes are, where I need to revise and what I need to put in there to make sure the students understand the concept that I'm trying to teach.

I always look at a unit now and make sure that it does flow conceptually. If not, then I rearrange to make sure I include ideas that build upon one another. I always make that a part of my science teaching and I want to incorporate the Conceptual Flow into other content areas.

Back to Assessment

The Conceptual Flow identifies the learning goals and forms the basis for instruction, but what about assessment? Teachers apply the Record of Assessments in Instructional Materials (RAIM) process presented in the next chapter to designate assessment points in their Conceptual Flow and identify the assessments that will form the basis of their assessment plan.

5

Plan Assessment and Instruction

ACT Portfolio
Phase II
Steps
1, 2, 3, 4, 5

Select or Design Appropriate Assessments Using the Record of Assessments in Instructional Materials (RAIM)

In this chapter, we discuss Phase II of the Assessment-Instruction Cycle where the assessment-centered teacher plans for assessment and instruction. The chapter describes the Record of Assessments in Instructional Materials (RAIM) as a tool and process that helps teachers establish their assessment plan based on their Conceptual Flow. We provide two examples of the RAIM: one based on the Conceptual Flow for *Earth Materials* presented in Chapter 4 and another based on the Conceptual Flow for the Science Technology Concepts for Middle Schools (STC/MS) unit *Organisms—Macro to Micro* (National Science Resources Center, 2003).

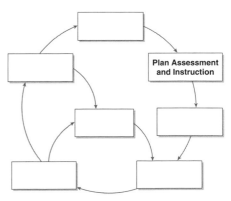

Plan Assessment and Instruction

"RAIM" and the *Assessment-Centered Teaching Framework*

The RAIM is Phase II of the planning process in the Assessment-Instruction Cycle. Use of the RAIM is aligned with the Assessment Knowledge Triangle at two vertices: Quality Goals for Student Learning and Progress and Quality Tools. At this point, teachers consider the alignment between the learning goals in the Conceptual Flow and the assessment tools for the unit. Assessment-centered teachers also determine the quality of the assessment tools (i.e., the extent to which the tools are appropriate for purpose, are developmentally appropriate, elicit the full range of student understanding, and communicate clear expectations). Teachers also consider the feasibility of the assessment tasks. The overarching question teachers ask themselves is: Will student responses to this task provide meaningful information about their understanding?

Purpose of "RAIM"

The RAIM process refocused my attention from using assessment for grading to selecting strategic assessments to guide instructional decisions towards a clearly defined learning goal for my students.

—Academy Teacher

> Although a teacher can develop a RAIM individually, the process is greatly enhanced through collaboration with other teachers and a facilitator. Teachers can work together to review the instructional materials and identify existing assessments and assessment opportunities. Discussions among teachers about the purpose of assessments and the responses that they anticipate from their students are more comprehensive when a range of teacher experience and content knowledge is focused on the task.

The RAIM process helps teachers, prior to teaching a unit, to develop an assessment plan aligned with the learning goals in their Conceptual Flow. Through a series of *ACT Portfolio* prompts, teachers identify which assessments in their instructional materials correspond with their assessment plan and analyze the quality of the assessments. Teachers decide (1) which assessment items elicit student understanding of the learning goals on the conceptual flow, (2) which assessments need to be revised or deleted, and (3) which assessments need to be developed to measure the identified learning goals. The completed RAIM provides a road map for measuring student progress over time within a unit of instruction.

Experience with the RAIM strengthens teachers' understanding of the pivotal role that conceptual frameworks play in expert thinking (Bransford, Brown, & Cocking, 1999). By organizing assessments to measure students' prior knowledge and the trajectory of progress toward the learning goal, teachers build their conceptual framework for Assessment-Centered Teaching. As teachers clarify the range of student understanding that each assessment will elicit, they also deepen their understanding of students' alternative conceptions. Alternative conceptions should not be quickly eliminated— they have a positive value for learners, serving an important function as the learners progressively construct more complex and generalized ideas. Assessment-centered teachers continually assess student conceptions to help them gradually construct pathways toward scientific understanding.

> You may have heard the term *misconception,* a term that is generally used to refer to a learner's vague, imperfect, or mistaken understanding that is difficult to change. We have chosen to use the term *alternative conception,* because cognitive psychologists, constructivist learning theorists, and science researchers have built a strong case for it. The term is used to describe an experience-based explanation constructed by a learner who is seeking to make a natural phenomenon or object understandable. The choice of *alternative* as opposed to *mis-* grants respect to the learner who holds the alternative idea— alternative conceptions are rational for the learner in a given context.

Role of "RAIM" in Building Reflective Practice

The process of completing the RAIM includes the following five steps:

1. Pre-think appropriate assessment points in the Conceptual Flow.

2. Match assessments to each point identified.

3. Select and arrange assessment tasks (pre-, junctures, and post-) in an assessment plan that enables the teacher to monitor student progress over time.

4. Develop expected student responses (ESRs) for selected assessment tasks.

5. Reflect on the coherence between the Conceptual Flow and assessment plan.

We illustrate the five RAIM steps with an example from the elementary Full Option Science System (FOSS) *Earth Materials* unit that builds on the Conceptual Flow we presented in Chapter 4. We then provide a briefer example of the development of the RAIM for a middle school unit, STC/MS's *Organisms—Macro to Micro*.

1. Pre-think Appropriate Assessment Points in the Conceptual Flow

A pre-think is a process used to help teachers access their prior knowledge and assumptions about a topic. In the development of the Conceptual Flow, the pre-think helps teachers think about discipline-specific content; in the RAIM process, the pre-think helps teachers think about where assessments can provide quality information about student thinking.

The RAIM process begins with teachers using a pre-think to identify assessment points in their conceptual flow. Teachers analyze the content chunks and consider how to embed both formative and summative assessment in relation to those chunks. Using a backward design process (Wiggins & McTighe, 2005), teachers first ask themselves: What would you expect a student to produce/understand on a post or summative assessment of this unit of instruction? Then, working backwards to earlier lessons in the unit, teachers ask: What knowledge should students acquire as they work toward the learning goals of the unit? Finally, they consider: What prior knowledge do students need to access the concepts in the unit?

During the pre-think, assessment-centered teachers place sticky notes on their Conceptual Flow to flag where assessments should be located. The flags visually indicate the points when the teacher needs to know what the students know (including possible alternative conceptions) before continuing instruction. The original Conceptual Flow for *Earth Materials* (FOSS, 2001), first displayed in Figure 4.3, is now flagged in Figure 5.1, indicating the assessment points that the teachers identified in their pre-think.

In this example, teachers decided to assess the big idea students should understand, "Earth materials can be observed, described, and separated into components," and the two main supporting ideas: "Rocks are a mixture of ingredients and have properties that can be described," and "Minerals are the basic substances that make up rocks and have properties that can be described," and they placed flags on those concepts. They placed flags on additional concepts they thought were essential for students to know to explain the differences between rocks and minerals: "Rocks have shape, texture, and size;" "Rocks are made of ingredients called minerals;" "Minerals are made of one ingredient and cannot be broken apart;" and "Minerals can be

Figure 5.1 Pre-think Flagging of Assessment Points FOSS *Earth Materials* Grades 3–4

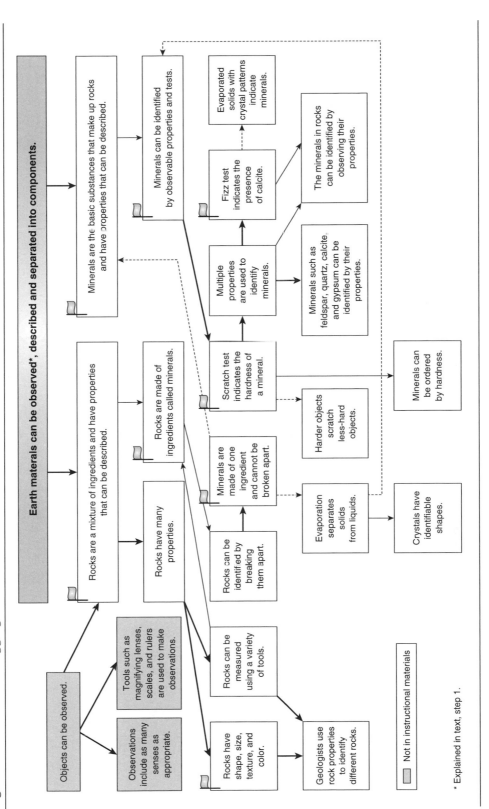

Not in instructional materials

* Explained in text, step 1.

identified by their properties;" and two of those properties involve hardness and the "fizz test." Teachers decided that their final concept, "The minerals that make up a rock can be identified by observing its characteristics" was a restatement of one of the main supporting ideas and could be assessed as part of a post-assessment.

The teachers recalled from constructing their Conceptual Flow that the unit included the inquiry skill of making accurate observations, and they decided that students' ability to use this inquiry skill was important for their understanding of the Earth science concepts. The team returned to their Conceptual Flow and starred the word *observe* in the big idea to remind them that the final assessment plan should include items to measure student understanding and use of quality observations.

2. Match Assessments to Each Point Identified

With the assessment points flagged in the Conceptual Flow, assessment-centered teachers begin matching their pre-think assessment points to the actual assessments found in their instructional materials. There are three possible scenarios for any given assessment point: 1) the assessment point may be supported by an assessment in the materials, 2) the assessment point may not be supported by any assessment in the materials (thus, teachers need to develop the assessment), or 3) the instructional materials include assessments for concepts that the teachers did not identify in their pre-think. Prompts in the *ACT Portfolio* help teachers address each of these situations. Below, we describe the process for each.

Scenario #1: Pre-think assessment points are supported by assessments in the materials. Selecting one concept at a time, assessment-centered teachers list *all* assessment tasks in the instructional materials that address a particular concept flagged during the pre-think. The list includes activities that may not be identified as assessments in the instructional materials but have potential to become assessments (e.g., journal prompts, discussion questions, or labs). Next, teachers consider the quality of each assessment task by determining what it does and does not elicit about student understanding of the concept. To analyze the task, teachers complete it themselves

> Assessment tools include the assessment task and the scoring criteria. The assessment task consists of assessment items. The task might consist of one assessment item, such as an open-ended prompt, or of many items, such a combination of multiple-choice items and performance questions. Scoring criteria are the guidelines for judging the quality of student work.

and then discuss how the prompt would elicit a range of student responses, including alternative conceptions. Depending on their analysis, teachers mark the task as "use as is," "revise," or "delete."

In our *Earth Materials* (FOSS, 2001) example, the teachers needed to assess student understanding of the concept that rocks have shape, size, texture, and color, and they identified several assessment tasks as well as some activities that could be adapted as assessments. The assessment tasks included a data chart for students to record data, and the team decided to use that task as is. The teachers also identified a notebook entry that could be revised to assess student understanding.

Scenario #2: Pre-think assessment point is not supported by assessment tasks in the materials. When assessment-centered teachers find no assessment tasks in the instructional materials for an assessment point concept flagged in the pre-think, they have two choices: to revise the pre-think or design an assessment task to match the pre-think. Sometimes the missing assessment can be adapted from an instructional activity, so teachers do not have to design an assessment from scratch. In our example of the *Earth Materials* (FOSS, 2001) unit, the teachers valued student understanding and use of inquiry skills as evidenced by the starred portion of the big idea on the Conceptual Flow. However, the instructional materials had no labeled assessment items that measured student knowledge or use of observation skills. Using prompts from the *ACT Portfolio,* teachers discussed the learning to be assessed and searched in the instructional materials for an activity that elicited student knowledge and use of observation. They then evaluated that activity as a potential assessment item based on its alignment to the learning goals and the student understanding it measured. The team decided that the activity had to be modified significantly to elicit student understanding about observation and noted it on their RAIM form.

In the event that no assessment tasks or activities in the instructional materials can be identified for a flagged concept, teachers utilize other resources (e.g., other instructional materials, assessment banks) to identify an appropriate assessment task, or they develop an assessment task. Development of a quality tool is a complex process, and when that became necessary in the Academy, our teachers were guided in that process with criteria for quality assessments (see Resource A, "Resources for Further Learning"). The new task is then noted on the RAIM form.

Scenario #3: Assessment tasks are included in the instructional materials but not in the assessment pre-think. The next series of *ACT Portfolio* prompts addresses a situation in which the instructional materials provide assessments for concepts the teachers did not flag on their Conceptual Flow. In this case, teachers decide whether the learning goal assessed is worthy of inclusion in the Conceptual Flow. If so, they add the goal and reorganize their Conceptual Flow, then evaluate whether the added goal is important to assess. If an assessment is needed, teachers decide whether the published assessment should be used as is, revised, or deleted.

The *Earth Materials* (FOSS, 2001) team did not find any identified assessment tasks for concepts they did not flag. However, the middle school team did, as we discuss later in this chapter.

To summarize this step, assessment-centered teachers identify assessment tasks in the instructional materials and align them with important learning goals for students. Additional prompts guide teachers as they analyze each task's capacity to elicit evidence of student understanding. As they evaluate tasks, teachers identify which need to be revised or developed for the final assessment plan.

3. Select and Arrange Assessment Tasks (Pre-, Junctures, Post-) in an Assessment Plan That Enables the Teacher to Monitor Student Progress Over Time

The final assessment plan is the foundation of the reflective *ACT Portfolio*. It specifies the tools that teachers will use to gather evidence of student learning and evidence that will guide teachers as they refine instruction and assessment. Therefore, the adage "go slow to go fast" is particularly important in the planning stages. Questions for reflection on the plan include: How does this plan capture the trajectory of student learning of a big idea? Is this plan feasible for implementation? To what extent does this plan include a variety of assessment prompts to enable all students to share their knowledge?

At this point in the process, *all* of the possible assessments for the unit have been identified. Teachers must now select from this assortment those assessments that will best monitor students' pathways of learning toward the learning goal. In an ideal world, teachers would use all student work as an assessment of student progress, yet few teachers have time to review every piece of student work on a daily basis. Instead, assessment-centered teachers must design an assessment plan that can provide them with appropriate and *feasible* data to monitor and adjust their instruction. Teachers use their knowledge of the learning goals and the flow of the concepts to select the most critical assessment points for deep analysis of student work.

The assessment plan should be designed to provide initial information on students' prior knowledge and a baseline for measuring progress, student understanding along a learning trajectory, and student understanding upon completion of the unit. A quality *pre-assessment* is aligned with the learning goals and elicits the full range of students' prior knowledge of the concepts identified in the Conceptual Flow. It also provides a baseline measure that can be used to monitor student progress during the unit. *Juncture assessments* provide formative information at key points throughout the unit, and they should be implemented when timely feedback can guide student progress toward the unit learning goals. *Post-assessments* are aligned with the unit's learning goals, and the content is aligned with concepts assessed on the pre-assessment to enable the teacher to measure growth in student understanding.

Identifying pre-, post- and juncture assessments requires teachers to review their backward plan (Wiggins & McTighe, 2005): What should students know and be able to do at the conclusion of the unit? Because there may be several concepts that students should have mastered, teachers consider which are most important to the assessment plan they will monitor: What concepts are critical to measure student understanding and provide useful and timely feedback?

In the *Earth Materials* (FOSS, 2001) RAIM pre-think, teachers identified ten assessment points. After much discussion, they designed an assessment plan that would assess student understanding at five intervals in their Conceptual Flow. They wanted a pre-assessment that would assess students' observation skills and prior knowledge about rocks and minerals as well as a post-assessment that would show growth in students' understanding of the properties of rock and minerals and how the properties help differentiate Earth materials. For their juncture assessments, the team identified three points of progress toward understanding that "Earth materials can be observed, described, and separated into components." These junctures included rocks have shape, size, color, and texture and are made of ingredients called minerals; hardness can be used to describe minerals; and reaction to weak acids can be used to identify calcite.

At this point in the planning process, assessment-centered teachers have identified crucial assessment points for the pre-, post- and juncture assessments. It is now time to select the most appropriate assessment tasks to measure the targeted concepts in their assessment plan. Through facilitated discussion, teachers review all the possible tasks for a selected concept and select those that will best elicit a

range of student thinking, including students' alternative conceptions. For example, for their post-assessment, the teachers using *Earth
Materials* (FOSS, 2001) reviewed several multiple-choice items and
an open-ended prompt to assess the concept that rocks and minerals
have properties by which they can be described and differentiated.
While the multiple-choice items were well written and easy to score,
the teachers decided that the open-ended question was a better
assessment choice. It would allow students to state their understanding of the differences between the rocks and minerals and to provide
evidence for their answer. Thus, the teachers selected the open-ended
question as the post-assessment task.

Assessment-centered teachers use the iterative reflective process
until they have designed an assessment plan that identifies pre-, post-
and juncture assessments that contain the best tasks for each assessment point. Table 5.1 illustrates the final assessment plan for *Earth
Materials* (FOSS, 2001). Note that not all the flagged concepts on the
Conceptual Flow in Figure 5.1 are part of the final assessment plan. If
feasible, individual teachers can add assessments for the remaining
flagged concepts when they implement the unit. In this example,
most of the assessments in the plan were found in the instructional
materials, although the curriculum developers did not label them all
as assessments. The only assessment missing was a pre-assessment
item that assessed student observation skills. Teachers developed a
pre-assessment by significantly modifying an existing activity in the
instructional materials.

4. Develop Expected Student Responses (ESRs) for Selected Assessment Tasks

With an assessment plan in place, teachers are ready to anticipate the ways that students may respond to particular assessment
items. Teachers generate expected student responses (ESRs), or
student answers that would be considered to demonstrate high,
medium, or low levels of understanding. Teachers begin by writing complete and optimal student responses that indicate achievement of the learning goal. Teachers then consider the full range of
student understanding of the learning goal and reflect on what a
middle- and low-level understanding would be. Even if scoring
guides or rubrics are available in the instructional materials, it is
extremely beneficial for teachers to develop ESRs. The teachers can
then compare their ESRs with the published scoring guides and
make revisions accordingly.

Table 5.1 Assessment Plan for *Earth Materials*

	Pre-Assessment	Juncture 1	Juncture 2	Juncture 3	Post-Assessment
Concepts From Conceptual Flow	Rocks and minerals have properties by which they can be described and differentiated. Quality observations are both quantitative and qualitative.	Rocks have shape, size, texture, and color, and they are made of ingredients called minerals.	Properties of hardness can be used to classify minerals.	Calcite can be detected with vinegar.	Rocks and minerals have properties by which they can be described and differentiated.
Assessment Tasks	**Narrative Item** Using observations and test results, students determine if an object is a rock or a mineral.	**Mock Rock** Use student journal entry on mock rock observations.	**Scratch Test** Scratch test to identify hardness.	**Calcite Quest Investigation** Fizz test to identify minerals.	**Narrative Item** Using observations and test results, students determine if an object is a rock or a mineral.

In developing ESRs, assessment-centered teachers are evaluating whether an item will elicit a full range of student understanding at their grade level and if alternative conceptions will be revealed. Teachers often find this a difficult endeavor for pretest and juncture items. For example, while students may have limited prior knowledge of a concept at the time of the pre-assessment, teachers still need to write an expected student response that reflects a high level of understanding.

Tables 5.2a and 5.2b illustrate ESRs developed by the *Earth Materials* (FOSS, 2001) team. The task for the pre-assessment and post-assessment (Table 5.2a) is designed to measure student understanding of the similarities and differences between rocks and minerals. The ESRs (Table 5.2b) indicate both quantitative and qualitative differences between levels of understanding. A high response includes knowledge that rocks are made up of minerals, that tests can determine the presence of minerals, and that there is variation among rocks. The low response indicates confusion about the role of shape or color as a distinctive characteristic of a rock or mineral or absence of evidence to support the ideas.

Table 5.2a   Pre- and Post-Assessment (Item #18) FOSS *Earth Materials*

A student found a pretty stone in the park near her home. She wasn't sure if it was a rock or a mineral, so she took it home to try some tests. Below are the observations she wrote in her field notebook.
Date: 4/16/08 *Place Found: Larkey Park* *Observations:* • *About the size of my fist* • *Several colors: brown, black, tan, and white smooth round pieces stuck in what looks like cement (light gray color)* • *I can scratch the black pieces with a paper clip and the brown and white pieces with a penny.* • *When I put a few drops of acid on the cement part, it fizzes.* *Conclusions: I think this is a rock.*
List at least three things from the student's observations that would convince someone else that the pretty stone from the park is a rock, not a mineral.

Table 5.2b   Expected Student Responses (ESRs) for Assessment #18

Expected Student Response

What do you expect students to know? Write the full range of ideas and understandings for your students.

High	Medium	Low
Student clearly notes the difference between a rock and a mineral by stating that rocks are made up of minerals and identifying at least three of the following properties to support the answer: • There are several colors in the same rock. • The rock samples have pieces stuck together; minerals have only one component, so you don't see different pieces. • The different rock samples show different scratch results. • Fizzing indicates that calcite, a mineral, is a part of the rock sample. Only a part of the sample fizzes.	Student identifies the object as a rock or mineral and identifies at least one of the following properties to support the answer: • There are several colors in the same rock. • The rock samples have pieces stuck together; minerals have only one component so you don't see different pieces. • The different rock samples show different scratch results. • Fizzing indicates that calcite, a mineral, is a part of the rock sample. Only a part of the sample fizzes.	Student describes characteristics of the sample (e.g., a rock cannot be flat, but a mineral can; or minerals have a lot of colors and rocks do not) but provides no support that shows understanding of properties of rocks or minerals. The student does not mention the following: • The sample has several colors. • Rocks have pieces that are stuck together and minerals have only one component. • Scratch tests of different samples yield different results. • Fizzing indicates calcite is an ingredient.

As we will show in Chapter 7, expected student responses are a preliminary scoring framework for the assessment task. Teachers will revisit the ESRs when they develop scoring criteria once they have gathered student work during Phase V of the Assessment-Instruction Cycle. In the example above, teachers later used student work to refine the range of responses and clarify the quantitative and qualitative features of responses at each level.

> There are two issues to consider when developing ESRs. First, when crafting ESRs, teachers must think beyond scoring student work simply as either "right" or "wrong" or "answers may vary." Teachers need to address specific content and determine responses that represent a wide range of student thinking. The second issue is the assumption that published instructional materials always contain quality assessment tools (both the task and scoring guide). It is important for assessment-centered teachers to recognize that evaluation and, if necessary, revision of assessment tools are critical to designing a quality assessment plan.

5. Reflect on the Coherence Between the Conceptual Flow and Assessment Plan

The last step in the RAIM process is a reflection on the coherence between the Conceptual Flow and the assessment plan. Teachers describe any modifications (e.g., additional flagging of new assessment points) to their Conceptual Flow and the rationale for the changes. Teachers also reflect on one tool (task and the ESRs) that was particularly challenging and predict whether the changes they made to the task will capture more effectively the full range of student understanding. These reflections foreshadow the analysis of student work (Chapter 7). Lastly, teachers reflect on their designed assessment plan (identified pre-, post-, and juncture assessments) and discuss how they will use the RAIM to plan additional assessments—especially additional juncture assessments—that would be useful while teaching the unit.

The *Earth Materials* (FOSS, 2001) team decided that their assessment plan (the five selected assessments) was aligned with the major learning goals identified on their Conceptual Flow. They confirmed that the assessments captured several of the concepts in the other five flagged points, so they did not see the need for additional assessments at this time. Because they had to design the pre-assessment, they noted the importance of paying close attention to how well it elicited student knowledge and use of quality observation skills.

A Middle School RAIM Example

We now turn to an example of the RAIM process for a secondary unit, STC/MS's *Organisms—Macro to Micro* (National Science Resources

Center, 2003). Like the elementary team that used the five steps of the RAIM process for *Earth Materials* (FOSS, 2001), the middle school team began with the Conceptual Flow that they constructed to represent their interpretation of the concepts in the unit (Figure 5.2). In this flow, the big idea for the unit is "An organism is a complete living thing. Organisms can be viewed from a macro and micro level." Two concepts support this main idea: "Organisms have common characteristics that define them as living things," and "Organisms live in habitats." The teachers also noted that the concept of scientific inquiry was embedded in the unit as "Scientific inquiry (abilities and understanding) helps us observe and understand our world." The team also added three concepts that were not in the unit but were important ideas to connect several concepts. These concepts ("Organisms can be single-celled or multicellular," "Organisms demonstrate structure/function relationships," and "There is a difference between living and nonliving things.") are indicated in the gray boxes in the figure.

The team flagged assessment points on their Conceptual Flow using Step 1 to identify appropriate assessment points. The team located 13 assessment points that would be implemented over several months of instruction.

In Step 2 of the RAIM process, the team matched their assessment points to assessments in the instructional materials. The team identified several assessment tasks for its flagged assessment points, but for the most part, the team had to find activities that it could revise to become assessments or develop new tasks. For example, the unit's post-assessment only measured understanding of the common characteristics of living things, so the team decided to develop a richer post-assessment and indicated so on its RAIM forms. The team also found assessments that it had not identified in the pre-think, including a black-line master to label the parts of the microscope. The teachers decided not to use this task in their assessment plan, because they preferred to focus on student understanding of the characteristics of microscopic life.

Step 3 of the RAIM process prompted the team to develop an assessment plan to monitor student progress over time. Monitoring the original 13 flagged assessment points did not seem feasible, and the team decided they wanted students to know five major concepts by the end of the unit. They listed these concepts and then back-mapped what concepts needed to be assessed during the unit to monitor student progress along the learning trajectory. After much analysis of the back-mapping, the team decided that the learning opportunities of this unit most strongly supported three concepts and decided on an assessment plan that addressed those concepts, as indicated in Tables 5.3a–c.

Figure 5.2   Pre-think Flagging of Assessment Points STC/MS *"Organisms—Macro to Micro"*

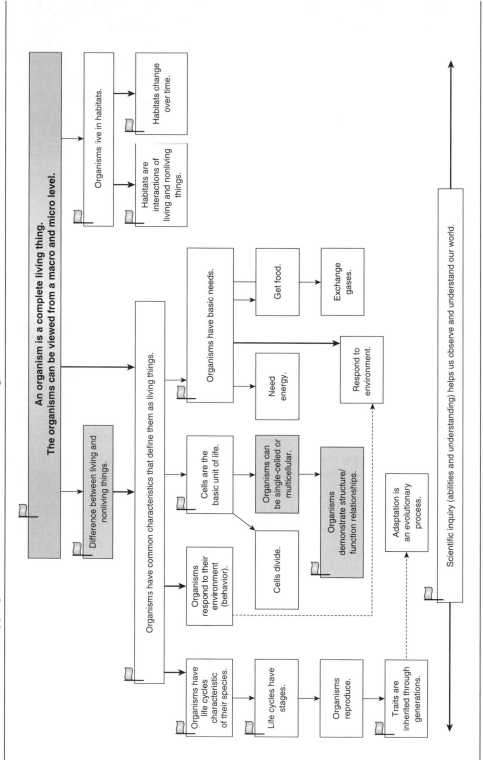

Table 5.3a   Assessment Plan for *Organisms—Macro to Micro* Concept 1

	Pre-	*Juncture #1*	*Juncture #2*	*Juncture #3*	*Post-*
Concept From Conceptual Flow	Living things have certain characteristics.	Living and nonliving things are different.	Living things have common characteristics that make them living.	Organisms have basic needs.	Living organisms have basic needs and characteristics that make them living.
Task	Modify end-of-unit task using dichotomous key to include characteristics.	Probe: Given a list of items, determine if they are living or nonliving and explain why.	Open-ended prompt: What are organisms? What are the characteristics of living things?	Write a summary of basic needs from fast plants, white butterfly, and hydra	Modify end of unit task using dichotomous key to include characteristics.

Table 5.3b   Assessment Plan for *Organisms—Macro to Micro* Concept 2

	Pre-	*Juncture #1*	*Juncture #2*	*Juncture #3*	*Post-*
Concept From Conceptual Flow	Living and nonliving components of a habitat interact.	Organisms live in habitats.	A habitat represents the interaction of living and nonliving things.	Habitats change over time due to the interactions.	Ecosystems (habitats) are made of living and nonliving things that affect each other and change over time.
Task	List of living and nonliving things; students identify which is which and indicate the interactions.	Student sheet 4.2: Make sketches of pond at the macro and micro level.	Pond observations; sketches of living organisms.	Change item I 18 from a multiple-choice question to a justified MC where students explain their answer about pond succession.	Repeat pre-assessment but change items for different ecosystems. Give scenario of a change in a nonliving thing; have students explain impact of change.

Table 5.3c   Assessment Plan for *Organisms—Macro to Micro* Concept 3

	Pre-	*Juncture #1*	*Juncture #2*	*Juncture #3*	*Post-*
Concept From Conceptual Flow	Science is a way of knowing.	Inquiry involves using basic skills.	Use experimental design.	Conduct a scientific investigation.	Inquiry skills enable us to understand our world.
Task	Develop quick-write.	WOW bug observations and two multiple-choice questions on graphing (H14–H15).	Inquiry Design Template for Fast plant investigation.	Compare mold formation on two types of bread; data collection, graphing, and summary statements.	Final performance task; student-generated question and experimentation.

The next step was to develop expected student responses for the assessment items. Table 5.4 shows the ESRs the team developed for Concept 3 (see Table 5.3c) for the Juncture #3 assessment. The team selected the lab in the instructional materials in which students investigated the effect of chemicals on the growth rate of fungi. They modified the questions so that students had to gather data, graph the data, and write a summary statement of the data—all elements of the learning goal for this unit. The ESRs for the Juncture #3 assessment display both quantitative and qualitative indicators of student levels of understanding of conducting scientific investigations. A high-quality response includes an understanding that there are relationships between the variables and incorporates scientific conventions when recording, graphing, and summarizing data. The low response fails to identify accurately the relationships between the variables and indicates a lack of understanding of scientific conventions when recording, graphing, or summarizing data.

For their final step in the RAIM process, the team reflected on the coherence of their assessment plan and their Conceptual Flow. They winnowed the 13 assessment points by selecting 3 major concepts to monitor, and their decisions helped the team determine the emphases for instruction as well as assessment in this semester-long unit. The post-assessment consisted of a task from the instructional materials modified to fit the instructional goals and items from other assessment sources selected to match the learning goals. The team was unsure if this mix of items would elicit a full range of student

Table 5.4   Expected Student Responses—Scientific Inquiry Growth Rate of Fungi

Expected Student Response		
What do you expect students to know? Write the full range of ideas and understandings for your students.		
High	*Medium*	*Low*
Student clearly connects the data recorded in the chart, plotted on the graph, and synthesized in the summary statement. Student accurately uses details and evidence to support the conclusions.	Student makes a general connection among data recorded in the chart, plotted on the graph, and synthesized in the summary statement. Student makes limited use of details and evidence to support the conclusions.	Student makes limited or no connection among data recorded in the chart, plotted on the graph, or synthesized in the summary statement. Student uses inaccurate details or does not use details and evidence to support the conclusions.
Student response	*Student response*	*Student response*
<ul><li>correctly labels the chart and graph;</li><li>indicates the relationship of the variables on the chart, graphs, and summary statement; and</li><li>uses specific data to support summary statements.</li></ul>	<ul><li>mislabels chart and/or graph,</li><li>indicates the relationship of variables on at least one of the three artifacts (chart, graph, or summary statement), or</li><li>makes general statements about the graph but does not support them with data.</li></ul>	<ul><li>may or may not mislabel chart and/or graph and</li><li>gives responses that do not include relationships between variables, or</li><li>neither provides a summary statement nor uses details as supporting evidence.</li></ul>

understanding and noted on their RAIM form to pay close attention to student work to determine if the assessments needed revision.

"RAIM" and Teacher Change

In surveys and interviews, many Academy teachers reported that the RAIM was a critical step toward becoming an assessment-centered

teacher. The reflective process of selecting assessments and anticipating student responses was an invaluable learning opportunity
for teachers. Carrie Green, an eighth-grade physical science teacher,
exemplifies the ways that the RAIM process prompted changes in
her understandings about assessment as well as her assessment
practices.

Learning to build an assessment plan on the Conceptual Flow.
Carrie came to the Academy with a great deal of experience developing
Conceptual Flows, but she had never constructed a flow to create
an assessment plan. During the Academy, she came to realize that
"you're looking at . . . the unit as a whole . . . you're seeing where
you're going and where you went . . . so it helps you see where to
insert an assessment. Because it's like a map, and this is going to be a
critical Y in the road."

Learning to think of juncture assessments as formative evidence
of progress. In her first ACT Portfolio, Carrie and her teaching partner
located junctures at the conclusion of major sections of curriculum as
summative assessments of a critical subconcept: "We said [students]
can't move to here [one subconcept] until they've moved to here [prior]
subconcept." But a year later, when Carrie and her partner revised
their assessment plan, they created junctures for lessons before the
culminating lesson in each module. For example, when they noticed
that density was interwoven through many lessons, they agreed it
would be useful to turn an early density lesson "into an assessment of
how much [students] understand at that point, since it's necessary
that they understand it throughout."

Learning to anticipate student conceptions when drafting the
Expected Student Responses. In Carrie's first ACT Portfolio, the
ESRs were written as statements of high responses only. For example,
for the concept, "Tools can be used to study matter," Carrie and her
teaching partner listed four ESRs: (1) identify differences between
observations and conclusions; (2) know how to use lab and tools;
(3) make accurate measurements; (4) provide a working definition of
matter. Carrie mused later, "We wrote expected student responses,
what you're expecting the students to say. The one thing that we did-
n't do was come up with what students might say if they didn't get it."
Carrie was recognizing the importance of anticipating students' alter-
native conceptions.

These comments from Carrie illustrate how developing an assessment plan using the Conceptual Flow and the RAIM can strengthen teachers' capacities to assess student learning throughout an instructional unit.

The researchers on our team also reported that the RAIM process helped teachers to become better consumers of assessment tasks. Assessment-centered teachers learn to analyze an array of assessments and select those tasks that most closely align with their learning goals. If tasks do not provide good measures of student understanding, teachers revise the tasks and scoring guides (addressed in detail in Chapter 10). These processes, supported by reflective prompts in the *ACT Portfolio,* allow teachers to think critically about the quality of the assessment tasks in instructional materials.

Academy teachers developed many insights through the use of the RAIM process, including the following:

- One Academy high school teacher realized that a pre-assessment on which many students missed almost all the items did not reveal important student prior knowledge on which he could build instruction. The pre-assessment items were heavily weighted with vocabulary words, making it impossible for students to share the knowledge they had that was not vocabulary dependent. When the teacher revised his assessment plan, he created a new pre-assessment that was less vocabulary weighted and more accessible to students. The changes enabled him to find out what students knew about the subject, not only their familiarity with the vocabulary, and provided him with more useful information for instructional planning.
- A middle school teacher realized that she was gathering a great deal of assessment data but was not gathering sufficient information on important concepts. She decided to make the number of assessment items for a concept proportional to the importance of the concept in her Conceptual Flow.
- An elementary teacher became aware of the influence of item format, readability, and graphics on student understanding of a task. Through the RAIM process, she learned either to select assessment items that her students could read, items with clear graphics and "friendly" formatting, or to revise the items. She recognized the importance of tasks that provide trustworthy information about student thinking.

The RAIM process also strengthened the teachers' ability to predict expected student responses and motivated teachers to consult the literature on students' alternative conceptions. For example, when middle school physics teachers planned to teach the concept that light travels in a straight line, they decided to assess students' potential conception of the "active eye" (that the eye "looks at" an object) before implementing instruction on vision. Life science teachers, when planning an assessment of the difference between living and nonliving things, included as a low ESR the belief that anything that appears dead is nonliving (e.g., a withered leaf), a widely held student conception.

Taking the Next Step

The Conceptual Flow and RAIM are advance-planning tools that assessment-centered teachers use before teaching a unit. When teachers are ready to implement their units, they need to reflect on the coherence of their learning goals, assessment plan, and instructional plan. They are then ready for Phase III of the Assessment-Instruction Cycle, which we describe in the next chapter.

6

Plan Assessment and Instruction

ACT Portfolio
Phase III
Steps
1, 2, 3, 4

Prepare for Assessments

In this chapter, we discuss Phase III of the Assessment-Instruction Cycle, when the assessment-centered teacher prepares for assessment and instruction.

"Prepare for Assessments" and the *Assessment-Centered Teaching Framework*

In Phase III of the Assessment-Instruction Cycle, teachers prepare for the assessments *before* teaching their unit of instruction. The Assessment Knowledge Triangle guides teachers as they consider alignment between the Quality Goals for Student Learning and Progress vertex and the Quality Tools and Quality Use vertices when they review their

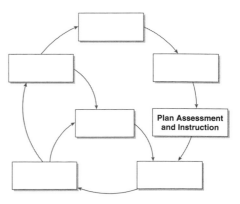

Plan Assessment and Instruction

assessment plan and strategize instruction to maximize student learning. By reflecting on a series of prompts, teachers are able to examine how the assessments can be used reasonably and fairly to uncover student understanding.

Purpose of "Prepare for Assessments"

We incorporated the "Prepare for Assessments" section of the *ACT Portfolio* to help teachers recognize the importance of reflective thinking in planning for instruction and assessment. This section of the *ACT Portfolio* contains a series of prompts that help teachers review and refine the pre-, juncture, and post-assessments they selected through the RAIM process and design appropriate instructional strategies to strengthen student understanding and performance.

Role of "Prepare for Assessments" in Building Reflective Practice

"Reflective practice is a deliberate pause to assume an open perspective, to allow for higher-level thinking processes" (York-Barr, Sommers, Ghere, & Montie, 2001, p. 6). Through the use of *ACT Portfolio* prompts, teachers are encouraged to think deeply about four steps *prior* to instruction:

1. Prepare for instruction.
2. Communicate performance expectations and plan feedback.
3. Administer the assessment.
4. Select target students.

1. Prepare for Instruction

The Prepare for Instruction prompts guide teachers as they anticipate the range in student understandings of the identified concept and prepare learning experiences that will help students progress in their understanding. When teachers identify alternative conceptions before teaching the unit, they can design instructional strategies and gather materials and resources to provide better, more focused instruction appropriate for a range of student understandings. For instance, if teachers are planning a density unit and know that some students will think that all heavy objects sink in water, they can design instruction that challenges students to confront their understanding, such as an investigation of flotation with objects of different masses and volumes.

Academy teachers found the following prompts helpful in Prepare for Instruction:

- What selected concepts will your students need to know and be able to do to complete the assessment?
- Select the two most important assessment tasks, and for each, predict the range in student responses. What will the responses reveal about the range in student understandings of the selected concepts?
- Brainstorm learning experiences that could help your students progress in their understanding of the selected concepts.

2. Communicate Performance Expectations and Plan Feedback

When the purpose and the expectations of assessments are clear to students, students are more likely to respond as expected, and their responses are more likely to provide accurate information about their understanding. In this phase of Prepare for Assessments, teachers review tasks and task instructions so that they convey clearly to students what they must know, say, think, and do. For example, for her plate tectonics unit, Yvette Jones decided she would share with her students the scoring rubric she developed prior to the assessment as well as samples of student work from previous classes that illustrated different levels of performance. Through her participation in the Academy, Yvette recognized the critical importance of helping students understand how their learning is assessed.

Prompts that guided Academy teachers as they planned how to communicate performance expectations to students included the following:

- What do students need to know about the purpose of the assessment?
- What are your expectations for the responses? Are students permitted to respond in more than one way? For example, can students use drawings to answer the prompts, and if so, how will you interpret the drawings?
- Will you share scoring rubrics (guides) with students before the assessment so students understand the expectations for good performance? If so, how?
- What feedback will you provide to students and other stakeholders (e.g., parents, administration, colleagues) after the assessment?

3. Administer the Assessment

The next set of prompts helps teachers plan how they will administer the assessment. Teachers consider learning goals, assessment demands, and the resources and materials that will support students in completing the tasks. For example, upon reviewing the language demands for an assessment, Carrie Green decided to include a word bank for her English-language Level 3 students and to have a native speaker translate the assessment questions for her English-language Level 2 students.

The following prompts helped Academy teachers plan administration of the assessment:

- What are the guidelines and norms for completing the assessment? For example, will students work independently, or can students share information with each other?
- What materials and resources may students use during the assessment? For example, will students be allowed to use resources from their notebooks or textbooks?
- What modifications (if any) do you need to make for students in special groups (e.g., special needs, English-language learners)?

4. Select Target Students

Selecting target students serves two related but distinct purposes. First, examination of the work of a select group of students enables teachers to "go deep" with analyses. Teachers can examine target students' responses to any given assessment in detail or analyze target students' work over time to monitor progress and identify students' successes and challenges. Second, examination of target students' responses helps teachers identify patterns that are important to assess systematically in a larger student sample or the whole class. For example, if a teacher finds evidence that an English language learner target student is misinterpreting task instructions, that teacher could reassess the English language learner students using both written and oral tasks. Analysis of target students' work is one strategy an assessment-centered teacher uses to ensure equity of assessment. It provides rich class data on students who represent specific student groups in the class, and these data become a resource for more systematic assessment of all students in the class.

The following two examples illustrate different purposes and uses for target student analysis:

Target Student: Example #1. One teacher chooses a girl with a hearing impairment as a target student, because he is concerned about her progress over time. The information the teacher gathers on this particular student is important but not relevant to a larger group, because no other students in the class have hearing impairments. The teacher uses his in-depth analysis over time to provide the student appropriate assistance and support.

Target Student: Example #2. Another teacher selects three target students based on the range in their performance on a unit pretest (a high performer, a medium performer, and a low performer); two are females, and one is male, a ratio reflective of the gender balance in the class. Throughout the unit, the teacher analyzes the work of these target students in considerable depth. If a pattern emerges that has important instructional implications, the teacher examines whole class work with equal care to identify other groups of students who may demonstrate the same response patterns. Note that this teacher's capacity to generalize target student patterns to other students in the class is enhanced, because the teacher used student performance on the class pretest to guide the selection of target students.

The following prompts guided Academy teachers in selecting target students:

- Are there student groups who are performing better, groups who are performing less well, or students whose performance puzzles you? What could you learn from the analysis of these students and their work?
- Is there a group of students in your class who may have learning needs that differ from the rest of the class? What could you learn from analysis of these students' work?
- After administering and scoring a pre-assessment, identify three or four papers that represent typical high, medium, and low pre-assessment performance. What might you learn from these groups if you monitored their growth over time? Could any patterns in these papers be assessed systematically for the whole class?
- Select three or four students as the focus for your in-depth analysis. Provide the rationale behind your choice: What do you hope to learn from each student? Will you use the target students to examine student work intensively for one assessment? Will you use the target students to analyze their growth over time?

Tables 6.1a and 6.1b illustrate how two teachers (third- and fourth-grade and eighth-grade respectively) selected their target students. Note the similarities and differences in what these teachers anticipated learning from target students. In Class 1 (third/fourth grade), the teacher selected target students who represented a range of performance levels and specific instructional challenges. This teacher wanted to understand what individual target students were learning and then design specific strategies to help *individual students* in her class. In Class 2 (eighth grade), the teacher chose target students who represented a range of performance levels based on pre-assessment performance. This teacher's goal was to use target student data to better understand patterns and trends for students who responded in similar patterns on the pre-assessment and look for similarities in performance for high, medium, and low scores from *other students* on the pre-assessment.

Table 6.1a   Factors for Selection of Target Students Class 1: Third/Fourth Grade

Student	*Characteristics*	*Rationale, Explanation and Questions*
Target Student #1 (PJ, #7)	fourth-grade male, low performing, writing challenges	PJ is one of my three lowest-performing students. He is a fourth grader and has not had some of the same early learning experiences as many of my other students, and I've noticed in particular that he is a weak writer. Because all of the assessments in this unit require written communication, I want to figure out a way for him to show that he is learning science concepts and is improving his writing skills.
Target Student #2 (MG, #17)	third-grade female, medium performing, eager to learn, hearing impaired	MG is a third grader. She represents the medium range of performance in my class of 20. I want to monitor her progress to determine if the "bridge" strategies I'm using are successful in helping her to understand science concepts.
Target Student #3 (HP, #11)	fourth-grade female, high performing, ELL	HP is one of my higher-performing students. I want to look at her work over the course of the unit to see if she adds significantly to the skills and knowledge she already has and if there are ways I can better support her language development and fluency.

Table 6.1b   Factors for Selection of Target Students Class 2: Eighth Grade

Student	Characteristics	Rationale, Explanation and Questions
Target Student #1	Male, low-performing on pre-assessment, inconsistent work	Responses from the pre-assessment indicate a low level of understanding of the concepts in unit on buoyancy (e.g., mass = weight of object, volume = something you measure, big things sink, small things float). Will look at other students' pre-assessments for similar responses.
Target Student #2	Male, medium-performing on pre-assessment	Medium-level pre-assessment score; knows that mass is a constant but confused about mass/volume relationship (size and "floatiness" of objects). Will other students have same confusion?
Target Student #3	Female, high-performing on pre-assessment	High pre-assessment score; understands relationship between mass/volume with respect to sinking and floating, knows that liquids can have different densities, says that air causes objects to become less dense.

Perhaps the most challenging issue for teachers in selecting target students is ensuring equity. The importance of thinking critically about which students can provide rich class data and making valid generalizations from individual students to a larger student group and/or the whole class cannot be overemphasized. If target student selection and analysis is to be a productive tool that supports teaching and learning, these considerations must be approached in a fair and equitable manner. We will further examine the benefits and limitations of analyzing target student work in Chapter 8.

"Prepare for Assessments" and Teacher Change

Using the ACT Portfolio *prompts before I administered the assessments helped ground me in my plan. I actually changed two activities after I reviewed the prompts to communicate what I expected from students on the assessment.*

—Academy Teacher

Planning assessment implementation helps teachers develop a strategic, anticipatory approach to teaching and assessment. As they responded to the reflection questions in the Prepare for Assessment phase, Academy teachers developed new insights. Teachers learned the importance of communicating the purpose of the assessment and the expectations of performance. Teachers of English-language learners realized that students may have difficulty interpreting a task and may need scaffolds, such as a word bank or word wall in several languages, or may need to review the task and task instructions prior to the assessment. Teachers also recognized that some students may have difficulty communicating their understanding in writing and that it would be important, for example, to interview those students to gain more valid information about their understanding of the targeted concepts. Teachers came to understand the importance of reviewing research on student alternative conceptions in resources such as *Making Sense of Secondary Science* (Driver, Squires, Rushworth, & Wood-Robinson, 1994) to better anticipate the kinds of student ideas the assessments might uncover. Teachers also planned how to provide feedback to students about their performance, including one-on-one conferencing, writing notes to students instead of assigning a grade, discussing with students how performance could be improved (for example, by including evidence from the investigation in a summary statement), and providing benchmark papers for class analysis.

From Planning to Action

Assessment-centered teachers have now developed and reflected on a complete plan for assessment and instruction. They understand the Conceptual Flow, and they have designed an assessment plan to gauge their students' progress toward the learning goals and planned pedagogical strategies to support their students' progress. They have identified target students as part of a strategy to conduct more in-depth analysis. Teachers are now prepared with a detailed plan for implementing pre-, juncture, and post-assessments and analyzing the students' responses. It is time to teach! In the next chapter, we rejoin our assessment-centered teachers as they interpret student work.

7

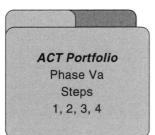

ACT Portfolio
Phase Va
Steps
1, 2, 3, 4

Analyze

Interpret Student Work Using
Scoring Criteria

As teachers learn a systematic approach to interpreting student work, they gain important insights into student thinking, the quality of their instruction, the quality of the tasks, and ultimately the quality of their learning goals for students. These feedback loops reveal the complex and iterative nature of Assessment-Centered Teaching. The Academy process of interpreting student work has three stages: (1) developing scoring criteria and scoring student work, (2) analyzing patterns and trends, and (3) analyzing data for target students. The first stage is described in this chapter. Stages 2 and 3 are described in Chapter 8.

"Developing Scoring Criteria and Scoring Student Work" and the *Assessment- Centered Teaching Framework*

The role of student work in the Assessment-Instruction Cycle lies at an important transition point in the cycle, where teachers use evidence from student work to draw conclusions about student learning and make

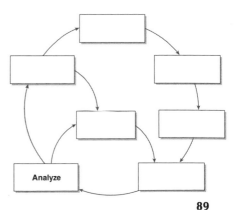

critical decisions regarding whether and how to modify instruction and assessment tools. Teachers begin Phase V of the Assessment-Instruction Cycle by reflecting on changes in instruction and/or the assessment that impacted student work and then move to developing scoring criteria. This process builds on the earlier planning phase in which teachers developed expected student responses (ESRs) for the pre-, juncture, and post-assessments. Assessment-centered teachers employ their knowledge of the Quality Tools vertex on the Assessment Knowledge Triangle as they design scoring criteria to capture the full range of student understanding.

Purpose of "Developing Scoring Criteria and Scoring Student Work"

Scoring criteria is a generic term used to define the guidelines for judging the quality of student performance in relation to the knowledge and skills that are being assessed. Scoring criteria differ depending on what is being assessed. For example, criteria may be used to judge correct versus incorrect responses, identify the presence or absence of certain features or content (e.g., checklists or point schemes), or judge the quality of the performance along a continuum. While Academy teachers developed a variety of scoring criteria, one particular type—a rubric/scoring guide (we used the terms synonymously)—was emphasized. Rubrics contain a set of score points with rich qualitative descriptions for each level of understanding. The levels on the rubric describe the full range of student understanding of the content assessed.

Developing scoring criteria is a process that allows teachers to reflect on the range of student understanding and use these criteria to interpret student work. To support teachers as they learned new ways to interpret evidence of student learning, we used protocols for analyzing and scoring student work. Our protocols were adapted from similar tools used in other professional development projects. (See Resource A for different approaches to looking at student work.) Our process links the expected student responses (ESRs) drafted during planning with the student work gathered during instruction and assessment. With the student work in hand, assessment-centered teachers revise their ESRs to create a scoring guide that captures the full range of student understanding revealed in the student work. Once a quality scoring guide is established, teachers can score student work and interpret the patterns to provide information about how students are learning. Developing scoring guides and scoring multiple sets of student work throughout a unit provide teachers with repeated opportunities to build scoring expertise.

The Role of "Developing Scoring Criteria and Scoring Student Work" in Building Reflective Practice

The first phase of interpreting student work is conducted using work gathered from the pre-assessment, juncture assessments, or the post-assessment. Like many of the phases in the Assessment-Instruction Cycle, developing criteria and scoring student work are iterative processes. These processes include the following four steps:

1. Review expected student responses (ESRs).

2. Sort student responses to the assessment task.

3. Write the scoring criteria.

4. Score student responses using the new criteria.

1. Review Expected Student Responses

Assessment-centered teachers begin the process by reviewing the expected student responses (ESRs) for the assessment item and evaluating whether they are still possible scoring criteria. The *ACT Portfolio* guides teachers by posing questions such as: How can I use my original ESRs as a starting point for developing a rubric to score student responses? Do the preliminary descriptors (ESRs) accurately capture a range of student ideas? Reviewing the ESRs reminds teachers of what they initially considered high, medium, and low responses to the assessment item. After this preliminary review, teachers are ready to examine student responses in a more systematic way.

2. Sort Student Responses to the Assessment Task

Sorting student work into "high," "medium," and "low" piles is a way for teachers to begin identifying the characteristics of student work that range in quality and understanding, even if the completed rubric eventually has fewer or more levels than these three. Assessment-centered teachers use their ESRs to guide their initial sorts in preparation for development of scoring criteria (Step 3). As teachers attempt to match the student papers with the ESRs, they make notes about characteristics of the different levels of responses. If they find responses that do not fit the preliminary ESRs, they can add levels to the scoring guide and note the relevant characteristics.

The prompts in the *ACT Portfolio* guide teachers toward the development of scoring criteria as they write specific descriptions of student performance levels based on actual student work. Table 7.1 shows how the *ACT Portfolio* prompts are used to guide teacher thinking. The left side of the table (*ACT Portfolio* Prompts) presents the questions teachers use to guide their thinking about ESRs. The right side of the table (Teacher Reflections) shows the rationale behind the prompts and the types of teacher reflection they are intended to elicit.

Table 7.2 is an example of a set of preliminary ESRs that Mary Schuttle, an Academy teacher, developed initially for the *Full Option Science System (FOSS) Diversity of Life Middle School Course, Teacher Guide* (2003) and the "characteristics of student responses" she completed as she sorted the student work. Note that her comments regarding characteristics of the levels of student responses include more detail about how students responded than she had originally

Table 7.1   Prompts to Guide ESRs Reflection

ACT Portfolio *Prompts*	*Teacher Reflections*
What are the general characteristics that define student responses at each level (high, medium, and low)?	This prompt asks teachers to be specific about what they expect from students in relation to understanding the concept and leads to developing more qualitative scoring criteria.
Review the high responses that you feel represent the most complete and accurate understanding. What are the characteristics of these responses? What makes them complete and accurate? How can you change your scoring criteria to include the responses?	Identifying specific characteristics of score points helps teachers to identify the qualities of a high response and helps to move teachers beyond thinking about a "high" response as simply the number of facts listed in a complete response.
Do any responses from within the medium responses indicate different levels of understanding? How can you change your scoring criteria to accommodate those responses?	By fine-tuning the criteria in this way, teachers are better able to capture the full range of student understanding. For example, the medium category might become two levels of understanding.
Are any responses difficult to categorize? If so, does this indicate a need to establish additional levels of responses? What are the characteristics of those responses?	This provides a chance to consider developing a four- or five-point scoring rubric (i.e., one that goes beyond high, medium, and low).

Table 7.2   *Diversity of Life* Preliminary ESRs With Characteristics From Student Work

Question Prompt	Preliminary ESRs	Characteristics of Student Responses
List at least five characteristics of living things. What do they need to have or be able to do to survive?	**High-level response:** Lists five characteristics of living things, such as growth, eating food, respiration, needing water, responding to stimuli, reproduction, elimination of waste, and being composed of cell(s).	Student does not necessarily mention cells as a characteristic of living things but includes all other features. May use "responds to environment" rather than responds to stimuli. May use nonacademic vocabulary (e.g., *breathing* rather than *respiration*).
	Medium-level response: Lists at least three characteristics of living things.	Student uses common language (e.g., *breathing* rather than *respiration*); lists common characteristics (e.g., breathes, eats, moves); does not mention reproduction, waste elimination, response to stimuli, or being composed of cells.
	Low-level response: Lists one characteristic of living things: needing food, water, and/or air.	Student lists anything that moves as living (alternative conception) or cites characteristics shared by humans (e.g., eyes, legs, arms).

indicated in the preliminary ESRs and will help her create better descriptions for the final scoring guide, which will indicate a range of student understanding.

3. Write the Scoring Criteria

After sorting the work and describing the range of student responses, assessment-centered teachers draft scoring criteria that identify characteristics of each level of student response. Generally, teachers find it easiest to characterize the high- and low-level responses and more challenging to capture subtle differences between high and medium and medium and low performances. Teachers often encounter student responses that are hard to categorize and challenge them to understand underlying student thinking. The *ACT Portfolio* prompts teachers to think through these issues with questions such as these: What characteristics differentiate a high from a medium response and a medium from a low response? What changes can be made to the ESRs to better capture these differences? How can the ESRs be revised to reflect more accurately the hard-to-categorize student responses?

Based on the answers to these prompts, teachers may decide to expand the scoring guide from three levels to four or more levels of responses. For example, the medium category might be expanded to form two categories: high-medium and low-medium.

There are many different types of scoring criteria (e.g., analytic, holistic, component) that can be used for evaluating student work. (See Resource A, "Resources for Further Learning," for more information on rubrics.) Regardless of the type of scoring criteria used, when Academy teachers described levels of student performance, they learned that criteria were more likely to guide improvements in their instruction if the performance levels identified students' commonly held alternative conceptions. For example, when recording the characteristics of student responses found in Table 7.2, Mary Schuttle recognized that students held the alternative conception that "anything that moves is living"; students who hold this idea may think that fire is alive because it spreads and wind is alive because they can feel it move against their cheek. (Mary recognized the need to incorporate the alternative conception in her scoring criteria (see Table 7.3).

> Instructional material scoring guides may focus exclusively on quantitative features of student responses without providing descriptive information about levels of student understanding. Critical evaluation of published scoring guides is as important as careful analysis of published assessment tasks. If necessary, teachers may need to alter or augment published scoring guides.

> Teachers need resources on conceptual change to help guide the design of criteria that can better assess student progress (American Association for the Advancement of Science [AAAS], 1993; Driver, Squires, Rushworth, & Wood-Robinson, 1994). They also benefit from collaboration with colleagues who can share what they have learned about student understanding through experience teaching particular content. When teachers better understand how students learn specific concepts and the contexts that best support this learning, they can more accurately predict how students are likely to interpret important ideas in science.

As a next step, Mary rewrote her criteria to provide better descriptions that capture more of the ranges in student responses. Table 7.3 contains her "final" criteria. Compare her preliminary ESRs, noted in the first column, with the final criteria, noted in the second column. The

Table 7.3   From ESRs to Criteria

Comparison of ESRs to Final Scoring Criteria		
	Preliminary ESR	*Scoring Criteria*
High Response	Lists five characteristics of living things, such as growth, eating food, respiration, needing water, responding to stimuli, reproduction, elimination of waste, and being composed of cell(s).	Describes five features of living things that go beyond the common features (e.g., needing food, water, shelter, and/or air) and addresses more complex features (e.g., being made of cells). Uses academic vocabulary where appropriate (e.g., *respiration* for "breathing," *reproduction* for "having babies").
Medium Response	Lists at least three characteristics of living things.	Describes three features of living things; the features are the basics (e.g., needing food, water, shelter, and/or air; growth). Uses basic vocabulary.
Low Response	Lists one characteristic of living things	Describes one feature OR indicates alternative conceptions, such as everything that moves is living, OR uses circular logic, such as anything that is dead is nonliving, OR lists body parts (e.g., head, arm, leg).

original ESRs were quantitative (i.e., numerical) and contain little descriptive information, while the new criteria are both quantitative and qualitative and help determine if the students understand the basic characteristics of living things.

To encourage teachers to move from a quantitative approach toward a more qualitative and content-rich approach to scoring, teachers need to build appropriate pedagogical content knowledge. Collaborative examination and discussion of student work with colleagues who have taught the same unit and given the same assessments exposes teachers to a wider range of student understanding and progress, helping them identify alternative conceptions and learning trajectories that they may not have anticipated or observed in their students' work. This systematic analysis of student thinking challenges teachers to extend their content knowledge and can be a powerful way to build and internalize pedagogical content knowledge.

4. Score Student Responses Using the New Criteria

Prompt and timely scoring of student work is critically important to ensure that evidence from student work can be used to influence instructional decisions. For this reason, we recommend that teachers score work immediately after it is completed and discuss student work with colleagues as soon as possible.

Using the new scoring criteria, teachers systematically score the student work to capture patterns of conceptual understanding and growth. They chart the responses in preparation for analysis of student performance.

As teams of teachers and facilitators score student work together, they can incorporate important assessment concepts from the *ACT Framework,* such as consistency, reliability, fairness, and equity, into discussions of the scoring process. Table 7.4 specifies the type of teacher knowledge that each *ACT Portfolio* prompt supports and illustrates how it guides the discussion of these concepts. Some of the issues raised by these discussions impact the actual scoring. For example, teachers may decide to have more than one person score a sample set of papers and then compare the scores, use anchor papers—student work samples that clearly define each level of performance—as reference for quality, and/or rescore work after criteria have been refined. In this way, teachers can better establish reliability and consistency of the scoring process.

Table 7.4   Ensuring Quality Scoring

ACT Portfolio *Prompts*	*Knowledge of Quality Assessment*
How can I ensure that I score papers consistently?	Teachers understand that reliability is a measure of the degree to which the same papers will be given the same score if the scoring process is applied repeatedly.
To what extent am I evaluating student work within the scope of the scoring criteria?	Teachers understand that ensuring fairness to students involves basing the score only on the explicit content listed in the criteria (i.e., not on other factors, such as length of response or clarity of communication, when not defined in criteria).
To what extent does the range of student performance reflect the opportunities for all of my students to learn the content?	Teachers understand that students must be present for relevant class instruction to be equitably evaluated for their understanding.

Additional information about consistency and reliability of scoring can be found in Resource A, "Classroom Assessment—General."

Mary Schuttle enhanced the consistency and reliability of her scoring decisions by assigning ID numbers to student papers prior to scoring. This ensured anonymity. Mary also used a set of benchmark papers as a reference when working through the stack of student work. But midway through scoring, Mary realized that her scoring decisions had changed; many of the "medium papers" she had read included some characteristics not captured in her rubric. Mary revised the rubric and returned to the previously scored papers to rescore them accordingly.

"Developing Scoring Criteria and Scoring Student Work" and Teacher Change

Academy teachers reported being fascinated with the evidence of student learning they uncovered as they developed criteria and scored student responses. Developing and using criteria strengthened teachers' capacity to connect learning goals with measurement of student understanding of those goals.

> Research substantiates the value of teachers regularly and systematically recording and interpreting assessment data (Fuchs & Fuchs, 1986; Little, Gearhart, Curry, & Kafka, 2003). Student achievement is significantly enhanced when teachers use an organized approach to formative assessment of student progress (Fuchs & Fuchs).

Academy teachers made gradual yet steady progress in developing quality criteria. Many teachers entered the Academy using criteria that focused solely on right or wrong answers, or they relied on holistic scoring guides that designated student responses as "complete," "partially complete," or "incomplete." But as Academy teachers learned to develop criteria and score student work, they began to see the value of criteria that capture levels of conceptual understanding. Over time, teachers developed more detailed, content-specific criteria appropriate to their assessment tasks and aligned with their learning goals, and they paid greater attention to patterns of conceptual development.

One example of this growth comes from teacher Connie MacKenzie. In her first portfolio for a third-grade unit on water, Connie used the publisher's + (plus), ✔ (check), and − (minus) generic scoring guide for complete responses, partially complete responses, and no responses when scoring student responses to short answer items. She did not analyze student responses beyond this basic categorization. By Connie's third portfolio for *Earth Materials* (FOSS, 2001), her criteria (see Table 7.5) contained specific information

Table 7.5   Connie's Scoring Guide

Level	What the Student Already Knows	Expected Student Response	What the Student Needs to Learn
RE	**Rock Expert** Student knows that the property of hardness can be used to classify minerals and that a harder mineral always scratches a softer mineral.	Student agrees that rubbing two materials together is a legitimate test for hardness. States that a harder mineral will always scratch a softer mineral. Concludes that because gray mineral was scratched, the whiter mineral is harder.	
RN	**Rock Novice** Student knows that the property of hardness can be used to classify minerals.	Student agrees that rubbing two materials together is a legitimate test for hardness. States that a harder mineral will always scratch a softer mineral.	Student needs to understand that because the whiter mineral is scratched, the gray mineral must be harder than the white mineral.
RO	**Rock Observer** Student knows that when two rocks are rubbed together, one will scratch the other, but can't identify hardness as a cause for the scratch.	Student agrees that rubbing two materials together is a legitimate test for hardness.	Student needs to understand that the scratch test is a way to identify rock hardness.
UF	**Unconventional Feature** Student writes that one rock scratched the other because it was bigger. Student thinks size of the rock determines its hardness.	Student gives some information about the minerals or the hardness that does not pertain to the task or includes an alternative conception (e.g., size = hardness).	Student needs to observe that rocks can cause scratches on one another and that size is not a factor in the hardness of a rock.

about rocks and minerals. In anticipation of the way she intended to use her scores as a guide for student learning, Connie inserted a column in her scoring guide that specified what additional information, concepts, and ideas students needed to learn to move to the next level of understanding. Connie's scoring guide provided her with information about conceptual development by addressing the same concepts over time, and it served as a student-friendly support for learning.

Many teachers are uncertain how to use assessment data as evidence of student learning rather than as the basis for grades. The Academy's iterative process of revising criteria and scoring student work led teachers to appreciate the value of shifting their focus from counting correct answers toward discovering evidence of student understanding through the application of quality criteria. As we will see in Chapters 8 and 9, assessment-centered teachers come to understand that the processes of developing scoring criteria, scoring student work, and using the evidence to make decisions regarding instruction are interwoven.

Next Steps for Interpreting Student Work

Once teachers have developed a scoring rubric and have scored student work, they can analyze patterns and trends in student understanding. In Chapter 8, we discuss methods of analyzing both whole class and target student data.

8

Analyze: Interpret Student Work Through Analysis of Patterns and Trends

ACT Portfolio
Phase Vb
Steps
1, 2, 3, 4, 5

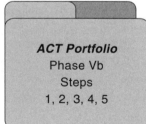

Assessment-centered teachers analyze student work and use the information from their analysis to refine instruction, assessments, and learning goals. In this chapter, we discuss two strategies for interpreting student work: analysis of patterns and trends in whole class data and analysis of data for selected target students.

"Analyzing Patterns and Trends" and the *Assessment-Centered Teaching Framework*

One of the more challenging aspects of interpreting student work is making sense of assessment data to understand student learning. Assessment-centered teachers look for patterns and trends in student work by using tools like the Assessment Record (described below), guided by their knowledge of Sound Interpretation from the Assessment Knowledge Triangle. Sound Interpretation is situated between Quality Tools and Quality Use on the Assessment Knowledge Triangle for two reasons. First, and perhaps most obvious, the quality of the assessment tool influences the soundness of teachers' interpretations of student work. Second, teachers must know how to best extract assessment information from data in order to draw valid conclusions about student performance. Assessment-centered teachers understand these relationships, and they use the patterns identified from analyzing Assessment Records to guide instruction (Chapter 9) and revise assessments (Chapter 10).

Purpose of "Analyzing Patterns and Trends"

Analysis of patterns and trends illuminates patterns in student learning enabling teachers to make inferences about student performance so they can adjust instruction and assessment to meet their students' needs. It's essential that teachers begin the analysis with a clear purpose, although teachers can—and often do—revise their decisions as they proceed.

While analysis of patterns can be conducted using many factors, in the Academy we encouraged teachers to think about these three: the who, what, and how of the assessment. The *who* refers to the unit of analysis: whole class or target students. The *what* refers to item analysis: whether to focus on individual items or clusters of items linked to particular concepts. And the *how* refers to the tools and processes used to analyze the data—for example, which type of Assessment Record provides the best display of the data.

Role of "Analyzing Patterns and Trends" in Building Reflective Practice

Identifying and analyzing patterns and trends begins with three questions that address these factors. The questions are interconnected, but separately they help to draw attention to specific issues teachers must consider when planning their analysis:

- Based on your learning goals, what type of information do you need from this assessment about student learning?
- What is the appropriate unit of analysis (i.e., whole class or target students)? What is the appropriate item analysis (i.e., items versus item clusters)?
- What type of Assessment Record will be most useful for your analysis and provide a feasible and efficient way to analyze student performance? What types of questions can you ask or inferences can you draw from the data presented in the Assessment Record?

Based on Your Learning Goals, What Type of Information Do You Need From This Assessment About Student Learning?

In the prior step of the Assessment-Instruction Cycle, developing the scoring criteria (Chapter 7), teachers reviewed their learning goals and identified levels of understanding for the assessment task. The question for teachers now becomes this: What kind of information is needed from the assessment to inform my practice? To plan how they might analyze the patterns and trends, teachers reflect on the *who, what,* and *how* of the analysis. In the examples below, compare the decisions a teacher might make for a pre-assessment versus a quick formative check on student understanding.

Who: For the pre-assessment, the teacher typically wants information on the whole class, while for the formative assessment, a teacher might decide to examine data on a few students.

What: For the pre-assessment, the teacher may decide to examine student performance for each item to produce a detailed analysis of student understanding. If several items assess the same critical concept, the teacher may decide to look at student performance on that cluster of items. For a quick check, a teacher might select an individual item for analysis.

How: The answers to the *who* and *what* questions will guide the teacher's decisions about how best to display the data. For example, if the teacher decides to integrate information across a cluster of items, it would be advantageous to group those items in the Assessment Record. In addition, the teacher considers the kind of data that will be entered in the record—quantitative data (e.g., rubric scores) and/or qualitative data (e.g., notes on student understanding).

Consider how Alison Hone, a ninth-grade Earth science teacher, thought about the type of information she needed from a juncture assessment. Alison was teaching a module on convection, and because convection is a foundational concept for other modules in her Earth sciences curriculum, Alison felt she needed detailed information about each student's level of understanding of several convection principles (e.g., density, temperature differentials, circulating movement) so she could refine her sequence of instruction. Data from the pretest indicated that students were struggling with the concept of density, causing her to add several learning experiences about this critical concept to her instructional sequence. She was now ready to examine the results from the density juncture assessment that contained multiple-choice items, an open-ended prompt about sinking and floating, and a concept map. Alison needed to make decisions about the *who, what,* and *how* of her analysis, and she used the portfolio prompts we describe next to guide her decisions.

What Is the Appropriate Unit of Analysis (i.e., Whole Class or Target Students)? What Is the Appropriate Item Analysis (i.e., Items Versus Item Clusters)?

Consider the decisions assessment-centered teachers make about the *who* of the analysis: Why might teachers choose whole class analysis? Why might they choose target student analysis?

- *Whole class analysis* helps teachers understand how well students in the whole class are learning. An assessment-centered teacher reflects on questions such as the following: How did my class do—what are the overall patterns of understanding and alternative conceptions? Which items were the easiest, and which were most challenging overall for students? Whole class analysis is a good place to begin looking for patterns and trends, and once some have been identified, the teacher can "zoom in" on individual students or specific groups of students to investigate patterns in greater detail. For example, if teachers discovered that 50 percent of the class was struggling with a concept about force and motion, they might want to zoom in on a group of high-performing students and analyze their pattern of responses to see if they were also missing this concept. Zooming in and out between the whole class and an individual student or specific student group is a flexible way to get a rich understanding of patterns and trends. Teachers can reflect: How did a particular student perform on this task, and how does this student's performance compare with that of the class or of particular student groups? How did this group of students perform on a task? Are there differences in performance for different groups of students?

- *Target student analysis* is an intentional and strategic approach to gathering information on particular students. There are two main purposes for target student analysis:

  (1) It provides detailed information about the performance and understanding of specific student(s) over time so the teacher can design appropriate instructional interventions. The assessment-centered teacher reflects: Is this particular student performing consistently on assessments that measure understanding of related concepts? What progress is this particular student making toward achieving the learning goals? What evidence is shown in the student's work that my instructional strategies are producing results?

  (2) It can be a feasible way to provide preliminary insights about larger samples of students; if important patterns emerge, then the teacher can decide to investigate the patterns systematically in the whole class set of responses. The assessment-centered teacher asks: How might the analysis of my target students relate to the performance of my whole class? Is this an important pattern that I should analyze for the whole class?

> What is the difference between target student analysis and zooming in on particular students in the context of whole class analysis? The target student analysis is intentional and preplanned, while individual student (or specific student group) analysis emerges as a teacher investigates patterns in the whole class set of responses.

When considering the *what* of the analysis, assessment-centered teachers decide whether to analyze student work by individual assessment items or by clusters of items that are conceptually related.

- *Individual item analysis* can help teachers answer questions such as the following: Which items were scored high (or low) for most students, and what do these patterns suggest about the quality of the items versus the quality of my instruction?

Teachers can also zoom in on patterns for a particular item that measures student understanding of a critical idea or concept in the Conceptual Flow.

- *Conceptually related cluster analysis* allows teachers to see patterns by looking at several items that are aligned with a critical concept in the Conceptual Flow. Analysis of item clusters helps teachers answer questions such as the following: How did students perform on items that relate to Concept A? Is there consistency or variation in student performance on scores for Concept A versus Concept B?

> Clustering items conceptually is an important process. Some instructional materials provide information on conceptually linked items, and teachers can use these guides to cluster items. But many instructional materials do not provide this information, so teachers should refer to the Conceptual Flow and RAIM (see Chapters 4 and 5) to select conceptually related items.

Assessment-centered teachers also employ "combination strategies" to identify relationships between items and students or between item clusters and students. For example, teachers can examine whether the lowest-performing students scored low across all items or only on particular items. Or teachers can examine which students performed the lowest and which the highest on an item cluster that relates to Concept A. Item-by-student analysis is a powerful yet flexible set of strategies for exploring more detailed patterns in the Assessment Record.

Now let's return to Alison Hone as she makes decisions about how to analyze student responses to her juncture assessment. Alison first reflected on the *ACT Portfolio* prompts to guide her decision on the unit of analysis:

- *Whole class:* Do you want to know if Class A performed better on the assessment than Class B? For example, what percentage of students appears to understand the concept, and what percentage of students appears to hold alternative conceptions?
- *Zoom in:*
  - *Specific student groups:* Are you interested in how the typically high-, medium-, and low-performing students score on this assessment?
  - *Individual student performance:* Are you interested in knowing how Student A performed on this assessment?
- *Target Student:* Is this assessment part of the "growth over time" analysis for a target student you are following? Would it be useful to analyze the target student data first, then see if the patterns are worth examining for the whole class?

Alison next used the *ACT Portfolio* prompts to determine the level of item analysis. She asked herself: Can some items on the assessment be clustered conceptually to reveal student understanding? Which single items are most critical to understanding an idea?

Finally, *ACT Portfolio* prompts ask teachers to pre-think their combination strategies—the item-by-student or concept-by-student interactions they will examine in their analysis. For example, will it be important to look carefully at the patterns of item scores for the middle-performing students? Or which students scored high, medium, and low on a key item? While it isn't always possible to make firm decisions about item-student interactions in advance, teachers find it useful to do some initial thinking about the patterns they are likely to explore.

The Academy emphasized starting with a whole class analysis to see what patterns might emerge from analyzing student work. Alison followed this basic approach, but she also knew she had several target students who were struggling with the relationship of mass and volume and thought that she might want to look at their patterns of responses. In terms of item analysis, Alison needed information about conceptual understanding and decided to group items that aligned with key concepts in her Conceptual Flow. Lastly, she considered the assessment items and realized that the student work would provide her with both quantitative and qualitative data. She was now ready to decide which type of Assessment Record would enable her to see key trends.

What Type of Assessment Record Will Be Most Useful for Your Analysis and Provide a Feasible and Efficient Way to Analyze Student Performance? What Types of Questions Can You Ask or Inferences Can You Draw From the Data Presented in the Assessment Record?

Using the *ACT Portfolio* process, assessment-centered teachers are guided through a series of prompts to help them identify the appropriate type of Assessment Record. For example, one prompt asks: How can I design a record that will provide a feasible and efficient way to analyze student performance? We provided Academy teachers with three samples of Assessment Records in the *ACT Portfolio* with the understanding that teachers could also devise their own records.

The first type of record is the Quantitative Assessment Record, which contains numerical information—a list of scores or numbers for assessment tasks. This type of record provides easy ways for teachers to record, organize, and summarize numeric scores and make comparisons of student performance based on those numbers.

The second type of record is the Qualitative Assessment Record, which contains descriptive information reflecting different levels of student understanding. These records, with rich descriptions that often include specific examples of student thinking, lend themselves to close analysis of student ideas and understandings. Qualitative records may also include a place for teacher notes and comments on student performance.

The third type of record is the Hybrid Assessment Record, which contains both qualitative and quantitative information. Using the hybrid approach, teachers have flexible options when analyzing patterns and trends. The hybrid record helps teachers better understand student thinking by using a combination of quantitative *and* qualitative data.

Examples of Assessment Records

In the pages that follow, we discuss examples of the three types of Assessment Records, and we use the Hybrid Assessment Record to describe how assessment-centered teachers use different methods of analysis (unit analysis and item analysis) to identify patterns and trends in student responses. Then we continue with Alison's story, illustrating how she used her Hybrid Assessment Record.

Quantitative Assessment Record: An Example

The first example of an Assessment Record is the Quantitative Assessment Record, which includes student identification information and quantified scores. The Assessment Record in Table 8.1 lists student names (or ID numbers) in the left column and the assessment tasks (e.g., specific questions, different assessments, or concepts) across the top row. Student responses are recorded in the cells. In this example, the scoring rubric is a 3-point scale, where + (plus) indicates a complete, correct response, ✔ (check) indicates a partial or partially correct response, and – (minus) indicates an incorrect response or no response. Data are displayed for only 4 students for ease of presentation and discussion, but summary totals are included for a hypothetical class of 20 students.

Table 8.1   Quantitative Assessment Record

Student IDs	Q1	Q2	Q3	Q4	Q5	Frequency of Score
001	+	+	+	+	+	+ = 5 ✔ = 0 – = 0
002	+	+	✔	–	✔	+ = 2 ✔ = 2 – = 1
003	–	✔	+	✔	-	+ = 1 ✔ = 2 – = 2
. . .	. . .	. . .	. . .	. . .	. . .	. . .
020	–	+	–	–	–	+ = 1 ✔ = 0 – = 4
Summary of Class Performance by Question	+ = 10 ✔ = 10 – = 0	+ = 20 ✔ = 0 – = 0	+ = 7 ✔ = 7 – = 6	+ = 8 ✔ = 7 – = 5	+ = 0 ✔ = 0 – = 20	**Total Responses** + = 45/100 = 45% ✔ = 24/100 = 24% – = 31/100 = 31%

Notice that this type of record helps the teacher recognize trends using different units of analysis by asking several questions: How many students received a +, ✔, or –? Which students had all +'s? How did Student 003 perform on the entire assessment? Did this student perform as anticipated? How did Student 001 compare with student 020 in terms of achieving the learning goal? Item analysis can also be used by asking slightly different questions such as the following: How did students perform on item #2? How did students perform on the conceptual cluster of items #1, #3, and# 5?

Qualitative Assessment Record: An Example

The second example of an Assessment Record is the Qualitative Assessment Record. Like the quantitative record, it contains student identification information, but the entries in each cell of this record contain qualitative descriptions (rather than quantitative data) of student performance. In Table 8.2, the students' performances on

Table 8.2   Qualitative Assessment Record—Juncture Assessment

Student IDs	Concept A: Mass	Concept B: Volume	Concept C: Density	Concept D: Reasoning	Comments
001	Doesn't know that mass is a constant—size/material confusion. Light/small stuff floats.	Confuses total volume with displaced volume.	Struggles with mass/volume relationship, sometimes M/V, other times V/M, other times 0.	Uses data to draw inaccurate conclusions on mass and volume.	Needs more specific work on mass.
002	Says "mass is always the same."	Gives example of how to calculate displaced volume.	Graphs M/V relationship correctly. Provides examples. Knows 1:1 relationship between g/ml.	Excellent use of data to support conclusions; uses graph, formula, and example.	What to do next? Discuss buoyancy?
...	...	...	...	...	...
020	Confuses mass with object size.	Unclear on constancy of volume: says sometimes light things displace little volume, but then confuses w/size (ships).	Beginning to see M/V relationship, but still confused on exact nature.	Uses evidence in unsystematic ways to discuss conclusions.	Do more work on mass-to-volume relationship.
Concept Summary	Half of students still confusing object size w/mass.	One third of students don't understand how to accurately calculate volume.	One quarter of students understand M/V relationship and can accurately graph it.	Almost all students need more work on using evidence to support claims.	See notes in other columns. Lots of work to be done!

assessment items are recorded based on levels of conceptual understanding on a continuum of ideas. (See Shavelson, Ruiz-Primo, &
Wiley [2005] and Kennedy, Brown, Draney, & Wilson [2005] for a
complete description of the assessment tasks and scoring guides.)
The cells contain information on the student's understandings of the
concept of density and its supporting ideas as well as their ability
to reason (which includes providing evidence for predictions and
explanations). Also, notice that this qualitative record contains
teacher notes (in addition to levels of student understanding the
column labeled "Comments").

The Qualitative Assessment Record can be analyzed in the same
ways as the quantitative record. Using the record in Table 8.2, a
teacher might highlight similar responses to gain understanding of
students' overall level of thinking (*whole class analysis*), focus the
analysis on *specific groups* of students to understand better how this
group is performing, or focus on an *individual student* to help the
teacher hone in on one student's thinking. The qualitative record
can also be analyzed by content focus, *individual items* or *conceptually related items,* or can be analyzed by *item-by-student interactions.*
We illustrate these methods in detail below for a Hybrid Assessment Record.

Hybrid Assessment Record: An Example

The third type of Assessment Record is the Hybrid Assessment
Record. As Table 8.3 shows, this type of record contains both quantitative data and qualitative descriptors of student understanding. As in
the other two Assessment Records, the students' names or ID numbers
are in the far left column, and the questions, items, tasks, or concepts
are labeled along the top row of the matrix. The row headers determine what is placed in the cell—quantitative information (numeric
scores) or qualitative information (descriptions or information on student responses). The entries in this record provide the teacher the
opportunity to analyze both the quantitative and qualitative patterns.

The example in Table 8.3 is a record of student responses to a
juncture assessment for *Earth Materials* (Full Option Science System
[FOSS], 2001). The items were designed to assess student understanding of the test for the presence of a mineral (calcite). The teacher also
wanted to reassess (and reconfirm) student understanding that rocks
are made of ingredients called minerals and that minerals have properties by which they can be described. The teacher's notes describe
student learning for these areas.

Table 8.3   Hybrid Assessment Record

Student IDs	Q1	Q2	Q3	Q4	Frequency of Score	Notes
001	+	+	+	+	+ = 4 / ✓ = 0 / – = 0	All + responses; showed complete understanding of how to use the tests to determine if object is rock or mineral and identify properties of minerals.
	States rocks made of ingredients called minerals.	Property of mineral is hardness.	Presence of bubbles indicates calcite.	Solid residue left from evaporation of liquid.		
002	+	+	✓	–	+ = 2 / ✓ = 1 / – = 1	Needs to know small amounts of bubbles do not necessarily indicate calcite; doesn't connect what evaporates and what remains.
	States rocks made of ingredients called minerals.	Property of mineral is hardness.	Thinks any bubbles indicate calcite.	It evaporated.		
003	✓	+	–	–	+ = 1 / ✓ = 1 / – = 2	Needs academic language for *stuff*; 2 – scores—needs help with calcite (doesn't recognize bubbles as indicator for calcite nor evaporation as a means to find a residue).
	Rocks made of stuff.	Property of mineral is hardness.	Notes presence of bubbles but not what they mean.	Dish A evaporated.		

(Continued)

Table 8.3 (Continued)

Student IDs	Q1	Q2	Q3	Q4	Frequency of Score	Notes
…	…	…	…	…	…	
020	–	✓	–	–	+ = 0 ✓ = 1 – = 3	3 – scores need attention; doesn't recognize components of rocks, doesn't generalize hardness as property, said both items had calcite.
	Rocks are chunks.	One scratches the other.	States presence of bubbles, so both have calcite.	Liquid disappears, calcite in both.		
Summary by Question	+ = 17 ✓ = 2 – = 1	+ = 15 ✓ = 5 – = 0	+ = 8 ✓ = 8 – = 4	+ = 5 ✓ = 8 – = 7	+ = 45 ✓ = 23 – = 12	OK with rocks made of minerals; hardness. Need help with amount of bubbles as an indicator of mineral.

Using the Hybrid Record to Identify Patterns and Trends

When assessment-centered teachers have constructed the appropriate Assessment Record, they are ready to identify patterns and trends. In the discussion that follows, we focus on Table 8.3 for our unit analysis (whole class and target students) and our item analysis (single items and clusters of conceptually related items).

> Professional development regarding the analysis of Assessment Records may focus on helping teachers recognize which trends provide important information about student learning and which do not. Looking for significant trends requires both sound content knowledge and pedagogical content knowledge.

Unit Analysis: The Who

Whole Class Analysis

Using the summary information, the teacher can conduct a whole class analysis by reviewing the number of students who are performing at a high–, medium– or low– level of understanding for each question and for the assessment as a whole. The overall class performance can be analyzed by calculating the frequency of items answered completely, partially, or incorrectly. In Table 8.3, out of the 100 possible responses (20 students × 5 questions), 45 percent of student responses were complete (+) responses, while the other two types of responses were less frequent, with 23 percent scored as partially correct (✔) and 12 percent as inaccurate/incomplete (–). This summary provides teachers with a general idea of whole class performance.

To pinpoint the specific concepts that students understand, the teacher can review the whole class qualitative data. For example, the data in Table 8.3 suggest that most students understand rocks are made of minerals, that one property of mineral is hardness, and that the presence of bubbles indicates a mineral. However, students do not understand that the quantity of bubbles produced is an important indicator of minerals, nor do they recognize how evaporation can result in a residue that can be used for identification of a mineral.

Is this analysis of whole class performance and overall trends sufficient? The answer to this question depends on the teacher's purpose for the assessment. Teachers may view the whole class trend information as a quick, formative check of understanding and decide that the information provided by the overall level of student understanding is satisfactory. However, additional important information can be gained from the record by zooming in on particular students or groups of students.

Individual Student Analysis

To examine individual student performance, a teacher focuses on the individual summary score in the column labeled "Frequency of Score" and reviews the column labeled "Notes" for qualitative descriptors of the student's understanding. The teacher can then reflect on patterns in student learning. For example, Student #1 answers all questions correctly, but Students #2 and #3 appear to have incomplete understandings of some of the concepts and answered at least one question inaccurately or incompletely.

Student #20 appears to be struggling with all of the concepts assessed. The teacher might also reflect: For what percentage of questions did Student #2 provide a + (complete understanding) answer? Which questions/tasks were more challenging for this student? Did this student perform as anticipated?

Specific Student Group

If teachers need information about how a specific group of students is performing, they analyze the data for that group and compare it to the whole class performance. For example, a teacher was interested in the performance of his English-language learners, particularly for question #4. He analyzed the results by looking at the quantitative totals as well as the qualitative descriptors and noticed that the students were scoring either + or – but not ✔ and that their responses did not include the principle of evaporation. He noted this trend to help him revise his instruction.

Depending upon the purpose of the assessment, teachers may want more information about the understanding of other student groups. For example, analysis of student scores based on gender and ethnicity may be important to consider and compare to the whole class performance.

Target Student (see also Target Student Analysis pp. 119–123.)

In this example, the teacher identified this assessment as an important benchmark to understand the depth of thinking of the pre-selected target students. Student #20 had a low performance on the pre-assessment, and the teacher decided to follow the student's growth along the learning trajectory. Analysis of the student work on this assessment indicates that the student is still performing below expectations in the understanding of several concepts, including that rocks are made of minerals, there are tests (bubbles and residue) for calcite, and that hardness is a property of minerals. Following selected students over time enables the teacher to reflect on what interventions are needed to deepen those students' understanding of key concepts.

Focusing on different items can also help the teacher find patterns and trends in student work. Examples of varied content foci are discussed next.

Item Analysis: The What

Individual Items

A scan of the summary row can tell the teacher on which items the students are performing the best (or worst). In our example, most students scored well (+) on items #1 and #2 and scored poorly on item #4. By reviewing the qualitative descriptors for these items, the teacher has information on the content of student understanding. Teachers can use information from specific items to reflect on factors that may have influenced student performance (e.g., the quality of the item, importance of a particular item in the learning sequence) and make informed instructional decisions about how to use the data from the item.

Cluster of Conceptually Related Items

The items in this example can be clustered in two ways: 1) all four items are analyzed to determine if students understand all of the tests that can be used to determine whether a sample is a rock or a mineral; 2) items #3 and #4 are analyzed to determine if students understand the specific indicators for calcite (bubbles and residue). Analysis of both the qualitative and quantitative data for these items suggests that many students are performing at a medium to high level for the four items but at a lower level of understanding for the #3/#4 concept cluster. Using the qualitative comments, the teacher recognizes that students are still struggling with understanding evaporation and residue as indicators.

Alison's Hybrid Assessment Record

Alison selected the Hybrid Assessment Record, as illustrated in Table 8.4, to record her students' performance on the density juncture assessment, which consisted of multiple-choice questions, an open-ended prompt, and a concept map. The record contains both quantitative and qualitative information.

Table 8.4   Hybrid Assessment Record—Density

Student IDs	Multiple Choice (12 score points)	Essay (5 score points)	Concept Map (10 points)	Notes
001	10/12 Missed all Qs on volume.	4/5 Volume discussion weak.	8/10 Volume isolated, not connected to mass.	Concept of mass-to-volume relationship is weak.
002	12/12 Provided details on all calculations.	5/5 Clear understanding of mass and volume.	10/10 Used all concepts, connections.	Understands relative density.
003	7/12 Missed all questions on mass and relative density.	2/5 Focused response on size of object, not mass.	6/10 Connected size of object with mass, volume = container size, relative density not used on map.	Not differentiating among size, mass, and volume.
. . .	. . .	. . .	. . .	
020	Data missing.	Data missing.	Data missing.	Not present for assessments.
Summary **- Total** **- Class** ** Average**	180/240 9/12	80/100 4/5	120/200 6/10	

Working with this Assessment Record, Alison had several choices for analysis. One choice was the *who,* and Alison first chose to zoom in on Student #1, a target student who was middle-performing on the pre-assessment, to give her an initial idea of the likely "average" student's performance. Another choice was the *what.* Alison decided to take a summary look at the multiple-choice responses but also look across all items pertaining to volume. She noticed that Student #1 scored fairly well (10/12) on the multiple-choice items but missed the two multiple-choice questions about volume and struggled with the concept of volume in the open-ended prompt and the concept map sections of the assessment. This pattern concerned Alison, because volume is a critical concept in student understanding of density. She wondered, "Is this pattern typical of the whole class?"

Alison zoomed out to examine whole class patterns in her Assessment Record. She found that the pattern was not common; however, she was still concerned about students like Student #1 who had scored similarly on the pre-assessment. When she zoomed back in on the responses of that specific student group, she found that these students were indeed struggling with the concept of volume. Like Student #1, they had difficulty explaining volume and its relationship to density on both the open-ended prompt and concept map.

Alison had one more important purpose for her analysis. A key to understanding density is to understand the relationships between mass and volume, and Alison wanted to know how students displayed these relationships on the concept map. Whole class analysis revealed three patterns that suggested three levels of understanding: understanding mass or volume but not their relationship, understanding the relationship of mass and volume of the object but not the relationship of the object's density to the liquid's density, and understanding relative density. Alison decided that the students with lower levels of understanding would benefit from additional density learning experiences to help them solidify their understanding of the concept, and she used this evidence to guide her instruction (Chapter 9).

Alison analyzed her Assessment Record in several different ways as she investigated different patterns in the data. Her methods illustrate the flexibility of the record. How it is analyzed depends on the teacher's purpose and the issues that emerge once the analysis begins.

"Analyzing Patterns and Trends" and Teacher Change

For many Academy teachers, learning to develop and use Assessment Records represented a paradigm shift in thinking about assessment. Many teachers had never analyzed student work for patterns and trends; thus, learning to develop and interpret Assessment Records was an important step in their quest to use quality tools in effective ways to improve student learning. As one teacher acknowledged,

"Analyzing the whole class was an eye opener for me, and I gained a lot of knowledge from that—from analyzing how I had taught and how we had assessed and what we were expecting that we didn't get." Many of his colleagues agreed.

One of the things I came away with was really analyzing student work, looking at it, and not just the items that were missed, or that they got it wrong, or just didn't get it from the book, but just really looking at it and seeing what trends were in the class. You know, if a whole bunch of kids missed this, but they answered it this way, you know, you look at the breakdown. I never spent that time on one assessment or one question before.

Whole class analysis is a place where I really strengthened in my practice. Before I would be looking at the individual student and giving them a grade and not really looking at the trends across my classroom and looking at individual concepts they might be lacking on and see if a lot of them are not getting it. So looking at those trends across the whole class has really impacted me a lot instead of just giving the grade to a particular student. It's like okay, let me look at all the work and compare it. It's great.

While most teachers focused on whole class patterns and trends, some teachers learned how to zoom back and forth between different units of analysis. For example, one teacher explained that "the whole-class analysis gives me an idea of what did work with the kids—these kids are getting this stuff," while individual student analysis helped her understand, "Okay, so if this is where this kid is, do I need to challenge him?"

Academy teachers sometimes used our Assessment Record models for organizing and analyzing, while at other times, teachers created their own approaches. Teachers came to see that Assessment Records can be designed and analyzed in flexible ways, and they learned to develop records that best fit their needs—the learning goals, the purpose of the assessment, and the criteria used to evaluate student learning. Our flexible model of analysis allowed teachers to tailor their strategies to the needs and contexts of their classrooms.

Through analysis of whole class records, Academy teachers came to appreciate the critical link between assessment and instruction.

The whole class analysis is very important—it really is a true guide for instruction. It's a guide for differentiation. It's a guide for grouping. It's a guide for a number of classroom issues.

I have become more proficient at interpreting the assessments through use of the matrix-grid where I lay out each student's response for every question. This has improved my ability to see the weaknesses in student understanding and therefore more easily guide instruction.

Teachers were very pleased with what they had learned: "I've got the whole group analysis down—looking for trends and that kind thing. I can do it!"

Target Student Analysis

A teacher may select target students based on their performance in prior units, on the unit's pretest, or during the unit. As we described in Chapter 6, assessment-centered teachers first select target students in the Prepare for Assessments phase. In that phase, teachers selected students for one of two purposes: (1) Will the analysis focus on an individual student's performance over time because that student appears to have particular learning needs? or (2) Will the analysis serve as an heuristic for generating preliminary ideas about student performance in a larger student group or the whole class? Assessment-centered teachers monitor student performance throughout instruction, and they may add to or revise their initial selection of target students as they refine their purposes for assessment.

The Academy placed particular emphasis on analysis of target student progress because few teachers have the time to monitor the progress of all students in the class. Academy teachers found the *ACT Portfolio* prompts helpful in reflecting on target student work:

1. Use notes you've made on each target student's performance on each assessment to analyze that student's pattern of learning. Construct a Record of Assessment using these notes.

2. Using the data you noted, what do you notice about each student's growth from pre- to juncture to post-assessment?

3. If target students were selected based on pre-assessment performance, focus on the pre-assessment and examine student
   work to see if students with similar pre-assessment scores
   moved or shifted in comparable ways as the target student(s)
   at the juncture and the post-assessment. What do you notice
   about student progress in the larger group? Do any obvious
   trends emerge from the responses?

Assessment Records for Target Students

A "growth over time" Assessment Record is constructed to record
data from several assessment points (e.g., pre-, post-, and juncture
assessments) in the unit, as illustrated in Table 8.5. This record,
adapted from *Earth Materials* (FOSS, 2001) includes target student
performance on the pre-, juncture, and post-assessments. Notice the
record of growth for Student #7. On the pre-assessment, Student #7
scored at Level 1 of understanding (inaccurate or incomplete level)
for both sections of the pre-assessment. At the juncture point, midway
through the unit, Student #7 had moved to a Level 2 understanding
(productive alternative conception). At the conclusion of the unit,
Student #7 scored at Level 4 on the scratch test for mineral identification and a Level 3 for the narrative portion of the assessment.

Table 8.6 lists the target students identified in Table 8.5 and illustrates how a teacher might reflect on the first two prompts above. In
answer to the first prompt, the teacher entered the data from each
assessment (e.g., performance levels); in answer to the second prompt,
the teacher added notes on student performance and understanding.

Table 8.5   Assessment Record of Target Student Growth

Student	Pre-assessment		Juncture	Post-assessment	
7	Scratch Level 1	Narrative Level 1	Level 2	Scratch Level 4	Narrative Level 3
9	Scratch Level 5	Narrative Level 4	Level 5	Scratch Level 5	Narrative Level 5
11	Scratch Level 2	Narrative Level 2	Level 5	Scratch Level 5	Narrative Level 3

Scoring guide adapted from *Earth Materials* (FOSS, 2001)

Key: Level 1 = off topic, Level 2 = unconventional features, Level 3 = rock observer, Level
4 = rock novice, Level 5 = rock expert. See Chapter 7 for complete description of score points.

Table 8.6   Assessment Record of Target Student Progress

Student	Pre-assessment	Juncture	Post-assessment
Target #1 PJ	PJ did not attempt the pre-assessment. I read the prompts to him, but he felt completely overwhelmed by the task. Maybe it was because of the writing task itself. No score.	At the juncture, PJ was more comfortable writing about science. He wrote quite a bit but did not focus on the relevant details of the question. His writing included unconventional features. He scored at a Level 2.	On the post-assessment, PJ wrote less but gave a more focused answer. He answered the scratch test question at a Level 4 and the narrative item at Level 3. He has shown considerable growth in this unit. I will continue to work with him to support his interest in science and improve his science writing skills.
Target #2 MG	MG scored at Level 2 on both parts of the pre-assessment. She wrote quite a bit, but most comments didn't address the question. She was both right and wrong about the rocks. She seemed to think that the color of the rock affected the scratches that were left.	At the juncture, MG was at Level 5. She knew that the rock with only a few bubbles was not calcite and suggested that the rock could be sandstone based on her previous experiences. She was clear that that the dish would have white crystals and correctly identified them as calcite.	On the post-assessment, MG scored at Level 5 on the scratch test, and Level 3 on the narrative. She still needs to build a better understanding of the properties that can be used to determine whether an object is a rock or a mineral. She has grown quite a bit in the unit, from a pre-assessment score of 4 to a post-assessment score of 8.
Target #3 HP	HP scored at Level 5 on the scratch pre-assessment and Level 4 on the narrative. She needed to learn that size is not an indicator of rock hardness.	At the juncture, HP scored at Level 5. She gave an ideal response, referencing both dishes and identifying the material as calcite.	On the post-assessment, HP scored at Level 5 on both parts of the assessment. Even though she knew most of the content before the unit started, the written responses and narrative items allowed me to see growth in her ability to show what she knows.

Scoring guide adapted from *Earth Materials* (FOSS, 2001).

Key: Level 1 = off-topic, Level 2 = unconventional features, Level 3 = rock observer, Level 4 = rock novice, Level 5 = rock expert

The Assessment Record enabled the teacher to examine how particular students progressed in their understanding as they worked through a unit.

In answer to the third prompt above, Alison Hone reviewed her Hybrid Assessment Record (Table 8.4). She was interested in analyzing her target student, who was middle-performing on the pretest, to give her an initial idea of the likely average student's performance. Alison analyzed the work of the target student (#1) and then zoomed out to examine other sections of her Assessment Record to see if the patterns of learning for Student #1 were common to other students who had scored similarly on the pretest. She found that the patterns of learning were similar, and she could generalize her understanding and interventions to meet these students' needs.

Target Student Analysis and Teacher Change

Many Academy teachers found target student analysis a useful source of information about the needs of particular students as well as the range of student needs in the classroom. Teachers appreciated the value of "going deep" with analysis of the work of a few students.

Looking at target students has made me more aware of the various needs in the classroom. Being aware has caused me to be more deliberate in my practices and to look for weaknesses or places where all students need more help.

Some teachers found that target student analysis was a time-saving tool for formative assessment of student thinking:

To do an item analysis on a class set of student work for 190 students or even 30 students is impossible. However, following three target students and doing an in-depth analysis of their work is manageable.

Before the Academy, I didn't appreciate the strategy of looking closely at three or four target students. I still wouldn't rely on just three (students), but what I appreciate about it is if you don't have a lot of time and you want to make crucial changes to a lesson that would benefit all of your students, looking at a high- a medium- and a low-performing student can help a teacher understand. Then at least you can reassess your lesson to give you a starting point to help students better understand the concept.

Some Academy teachers initially questioned the value of target student analysis, but as they gained experience, they came to understand target student analysis not as a replacement for whole class analysis but rather an additional tool that can enhance a teacher's understanding of student performance. Yvette, for example, was initially concerned that target student analysis could misrepresent patterns in the whole class.

What if I'm a teacher that only chooses three high students and end up catering to a certain population? My fear is that the needs of many would be missed because I focused on the needs of a few students.

But her views shifted over time:

The unit is large and so are the tests that we created. The tests were very detailed to reflect the concepts in the unit that built on one another. . . . and looking at three students is more feasible in the short run than looking at the work of all 90 of my students. That's something that has changed for me. I think, as a teacher, it would be my responsibility to then later on look at the entire class to see if the patterns I thought I observed do in fact ring true . . . to check to see if my sample students mirror the larger population of the students that I teach.

When Academy teachers gathered target student evidence throughout a unit of instruction, they discovered the value of analyzing target student progress to gain a deeper understanding of how students develop knowledge of key concepts. As one teacher stated, it is "critical that I do the target student selection and follow them along the whole entire year." Another teacher commented,

Rather than relying on impressions or my opinion to assess student learning[,] I am . . . using the [Academy's] processes . . . to take my analyses deeper. I would not have gone into the depth required to really guide my instruction. I particularly think following 3 students was valuable.

Benefits of Interpreting Student Work

Analyzing student work is a complex undertaking, and assessment-centered teachers benefit from working with others in collaborative settings. As they respond to the portfolio prompts together, teachers come to appreciate the importance of the *who, what,* and *how* decisions. When colleagues have different ideas about the analysis, teachers come to appreciate the flexibility of the Assessment Records, and those conversations deepen teachers' capacities to analyze student work in meaningful ways.

Possibilities for collaboration include within-school settings (e.g., grade-level partnerships or grade-level meetings), within-district communities, or cross-district communities. We found that "grade-level buddies"—teachers collaboratively teaching the same units within schools or districts—are a particularly useful support for teachers' growing expertise with interpretation of student work. Working with grade-level partners, the iterative processes of criteria development, scoring, whole class analysis, and target student analysis give teachers many opportunities to reflect on and revise their understanding of student learning. From data generated by the analysis, assessment-centered teachers then use evidence to improve instruction (Chapter 9) or to revise assessments (Chapter 10).

9

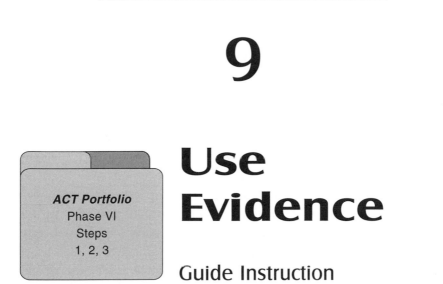

ACT Portfolio
Phase VI
Steps
1, 2, 3

Use Evidence

Guide Instruction

Assessment-centered teachers use evidence from student work to guide instruction, provide feedback to students, and refine assessment tools. In this chapter, we discuss how teachers use the evidence from student work to guide their instruction and provide feedback. Refining assessment tools is addressed in Chapter 10.

"Use Evidence to Guide Instruction" and the *Assessment-Centered Teaching Framework*

As teachers begin the "Use Evidence" phase of the Assessment-Instruction Cycle, they reach an important crossroad in the journey to improving their instruction and assessment practices. Teachers have completed their analysis of the student work and can now use this information in formative ways to support student learning. Analysis of evidence may lead teachers to reconsider learning goals, re-evaluate their teaching and their instructional materials, and/or revise their assessments and scoring guides.

Knowledge of Quality Use on the Assessment Knowledge Triangle is important as teachers consider how the evidence from student work serves as a guide for instructional improvements and provides the basis for constructive feedback to students. Teachers rely upon their understanding of Sound Interpretation to address specific issues in student learning, such as persistent alternative conceptions, incomplete understanding of content, and unclear or inappropriate expectations for students.

Purpose of "Use Evidence to Guide Instruction"

The central purpose of analyzing student work is to provide teachers with *assessment-based* evidence about student learning to guide instructional decisions. Assessment-centered teachers have gathered evidence of their student learning by scoring student work and creating Assessment Records to identify patterns and trends for the whole class as well as for targeted students or specific student groups. By reviewing this evidence before a unit of instruction is completed, teachers consider the effectiveness of instructional materials as well as their teaching practices in a timely manner.

Role of "Use Evidence to Guide Instruction" in Building Reflective Practice

Assessment-centered teachers use student evidence to make instructional decisions—for immediate as well as for future plans. For example, they may make immediate revisions in their instruction, or they may make revisions in their plan for teaching the same unit with the next set of students, teaching the next unit with the same class, or even teaching the unit next year. The *ACT Portfolio* provides three steps for reflection.

1. Identify general patterns in assessment results.
2. Identify specific revisions in instruction.
3. Plan feedback to students.

1. Identify General Patterns in Assessment Results

The first set of *ACT Portfolio* prompts asks teachers to focus on general patterns of student-learning problems, or alternative conceptions and to consider interventions that could be made to address those learning needs.

- Based on patterns you may have recognized through the analysis of student work, what interventions could you use to follow up in your instruction?
- Based on the trends that you have observed, what changes or augmentations to instruction would be helpful for your students? Consider the integrity of the Conceptual Flow, sequences for learning, and the variety and purpose of activities. Cite the evidence from student work used to guide your decisions.

For example, Academy teachers using the *Plate Tectonics: The Way the Earth Works* (Cuff, 2002) unit analyzed student work from the pre-assessment that revealed that some students held naïve notions about Earth science concepts. Many student ideas were on target: identifying the layers of the Earth, attributing movement of magma to convection currents, knowing that mountains are formed by plates coming together, and knowing that the sea floor is spreading. However, some student ideas were erroneous: weather is caused by changes in the Earth's core, valleys are caused by tectonic plates moving apart, volcanic eruptions are caused by forces in the Earth's core, and the core of the Earth is as hot as the sun. This information about student thinking helped to inform the teachers about the instructional emphases needed on specific subconcepts to help students expand and revise their initial ideas and alternative conceptions about plate tectonics.

2. Identify Specific Revisions in Instruction

After reviewing the patterns and trends in learning, a teacher then works to address the "what next?" in instruction. A second set of reflective prompts encourages teachers to focus on the specific aspects of instruction that might need revision by considering the following:

- The Conceptual Flow: Are "miniconcepts" needed to build a bridge between major concepts?
- Learning sequences for a particular concept: Do the activities address student understanding? How does the order of the

activities in the instructional materials build student understanding? Should other activities be incorporated to challenge student thinking? How do the questions promote deep student thinking?

- Selection of activities: Do all students have access and the opportunity to engage at their level of understanding? How do the activities help students confront and revise their alternative conceptions?

Assessment-centered teachers use assessment information to consider how student differences should be addressed when designing interventions. For example, which research-based classroom strategies (Marzano, 2001) are effective for particular types of learners? What modifications can be made for English-language learners to make the instruction accessible and still maintain the rigor of the content? What activities are most effective for the visual or kinesthetic learner?

Consider an example of the revisions to instruction that teachers made after reflecting on the second set of prompts. Carrie Green and her teaching partner, Juan, initially constructed their Conceptual Flow (shown in Figure 9.1) before teaching *Properties of Matter* (National Science Resources Center, 2000). "We looked more at whether or not the entire unit flowed, rather than looking at (specific) ideas and whether or not they repeated themselves, or were necessary [to re-emphasize] throughout the unit." The teachers closely aligned their Conceptual Flow to the flow that existed in the instructional materials. In other words, they did not consider rearrangement of the introduction of concepts, nor were they concerned in the first round about matching concepts to the state's standards.

After teaching the semester-long unit and analyzing student work from each assessment, Carrie and Juan decided, based on evidence in the student work, to focus on fewer concepts to make the unit more cohesive. Carrie reflected, "It was then that we decided to look more closely at our conceptual flow and make sure we were addressing the important threads throughout the entire unit." As they reviewed their Conceptual Flow and the student work, they discovered that understanding density was foundational for understanding many of the other concepts in the unit. They also analyzed state standards and identified the need to include concepts related to the periodic table.

Their revised Conceptual Flow is shown in Figure 9.2. Notice that concepts involving pure substances and mixtures were removed (to be taught in another unit) and that additional concepts about the structure of elements and the periodic table were added. To include these additional concepts, Carrie and Juan supplemented the STC/MS

Figure 9.1   STC/MS *Properties of Matter* Conceptual Flow Round I

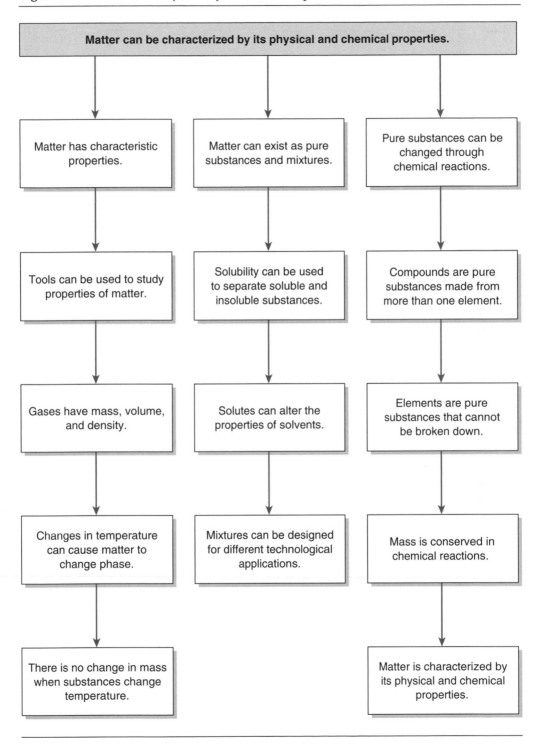

Figure 9.2   STC/MS *Properties of Matter* Conceptual Flow Round II

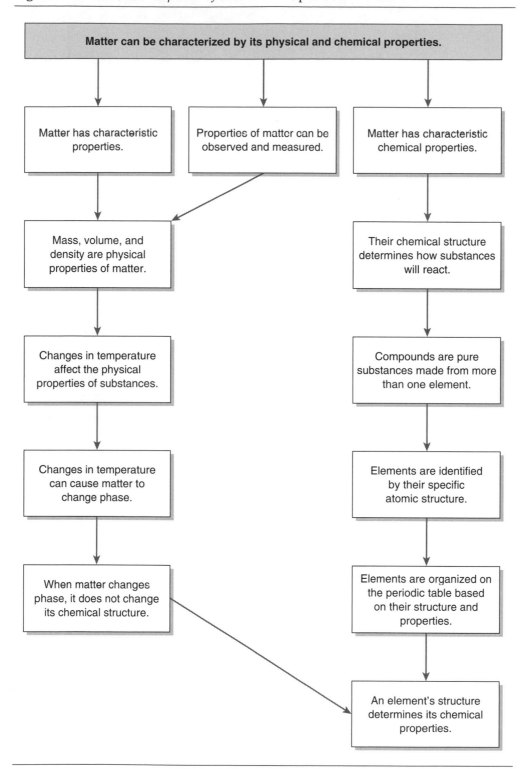

lessons with teacher-created materials. Their adjustments for instruction served better to provide coherence to the unit based on the learning goals they established for their students and had the added benefit of helping students meet state standards. In changing their Conceptual Flow, the teachers also had to change their assessment plan. A discussion of these changes is found in Chapter 10.

Academy teachers utilized a variety of instructional strategies in their quest to improve student learning, as appropriate to their units and their students' needs. Illustrative examples of their best teaching practices include the following:

- Using a "backward design" for lesson planning to identify key concepts for student understanding
- Engaging students in active learning to reveal and build on their prior understanding of a concept
- Designing questions (and expected student responses) to probe student understanding more deeply
- Using targeted, open-ended questions to encourage student discourse and the discussion of ideas
- Providing additional experiences when necessary to challenge student conceptions

Academy teachers developed these strategies based on their understanding of the interconnected nature of instruction and assessment. They learned that questioning strategies encourage reflection that helps students learn and, in turn, help teachers assess student understanding. During a whole class discussion, questions such as What makes you think this? Explain what you mean by. . . . What is your evidence for . . . ? can expose the specific reasons behind students' struggles with ideas, new and old. In small group work, probing questions can help students clarify and extend or redirect their thinking. Similar questions in informal interviews with individual students can uncover conceptual confusions while challenging students to formulate and revise their conceptions.

Once student thinking is revealed, assessment-centered teachers use various techniques to continue to probe the student's line of reasoning and help the student construct understandings that are more scientifically sound. Some structures for building new understandings include discourse circles, think-pair-share discussions, whiteboards to record group thinking, and poster presentations.

Teachers can also design alternative student investigations in which the student generates and interprets new evidence to help build a more complete and accurate understanding of the concept. For example, students struggling to accept the idea that gases have mass may need evidence that mass can be measured. One teacher explored this topic using several modalities, including digital and Internet resources and informational text, to help students access alternate ways of understanding the concept. The students were able to manipulate gases in ways that allowed them to measure the mass of gases and deepen their understanding that gases are indeed substances composed of atoms.

Finally, applying a concept to solving a problem in a new setting can be another effective way to challenge student thinking. For example, students can calculate the mass of objects of varying sizes to develop their understanding of the relationship between mass and volume. These strategies elicit the reasoning behind student conceptions and enable learners to make evaluative comparisons among different viewpoints. Critical thinking and debating skills are essential for students to be able to "do science" and gain a deeper understanding about the nature of scientific endeavors.

3. Plan Feedback to Students

The third set of *ACT Portfolio* prompts helps teachers plan how best to provide students with feedback on their learning. Teachers consider the following:

- How might you share scoring criteria so that students better understand what is expected of them?
- What kind of feedback can you provide to students about their performance on the assessment? Explain and provide examples of the feedback you might consider providing.
- What kind of feedback can you provide each target student about that student's performance on the assessment if it is different from that of the whole class? Provide examples of how you might do this.
- What conceptual information might you add to the criteria so that students know what they need to progress further?

Academy teachers provided students with various types of feedback on their learning and progress. For example, Connie MacKenzie indicated what students needed to do to progress in her *Earth Materials* (Full Option Science Systems [FOSS], 2001) rubric (Table 7.5). Another Academy teacher developed the rubric in Table 9.1 to help his students demonstrate their knowledge of electrical circuits. His

Table 9.1   Improving Student Feedback

Level	What the student currently knows and can do	What the student needs to do to move up to the next level
5	Student response correctly states what will happen in this case and why, then generalizes to other types of circuits. For example, the bulb will go out because the current cannot flow between the positive and negative poles of the battery. In series circuits, removing a bulb will prevent all current flow because there is only one path between the poles. In parallel circuits, removing a bulb will allow all the current to flow through the remaining path(s) between the poles.	
4	Student response correctly states what will happen in this case and why. For example, the other bulb will go out because when you remove the bulb in a series circuit, there is no way for the force to get from one pole of the battery to the other. Everything needs to be connected; there can't be an open circuit.	Student needs to state a general principle that would apply to objects in general (e.g., different types of circuits behave differently).
3	Student response justifies an answer (correct or incorrect) by recalling a similar experience or using what they have been told should happen. For example, the bulb will go out because when we did this in class, that is what happened.	Student needs to use a scientific relationship to explain the answer, not just state an experience they have had before or a memorized fact.
2	Student response justifies an answer (correct or incorrect) by recalling a similar experience or using what they have been told should happen, but the experience or recollection is not germane to this question. For example, putting a magnet close to the bulb would cause the light to come back on.	Student needs to understand evidence and explain what it means.
1	Student merely states an answer without explanation. For example, the bulb(s) will go out.	Student needs to justify (explain) answer in some way
0	The student left the response blank or the response cannot be interpreted.	Student needs to respond to the question.

rubric was organized as progressive levels of "what the student can already do" along with guidance—for him as well as the student—about how to progress to the next level.

As teachers become more experienced with a particular science content area, they gather ideas and resources for supplementing instruction to support student learning. Using evidence from assessments helps teachers to target specific instructional goals and identify appropriate interventions to help students on their path to understanding.

"Use Evidence to Guide Instruction" and Teacher Change

When Academy teachers started the project, many viewed assessment data as the grades in their grade book or the student scores on state accountability tests, and they saw little instructional value in these sources of information. If they administered a pre-assessment at the beginning of a unit, they often ignored it as a source of information for guiding instruction. Posttests were usually given as summative measures for purposes of grading. Overall, even if teachers recognized the value of student data to inform their instruction, they usually felt they had limited time to dwell on the information in assessments before moving on to the next lesson, the next module, or the next chapter in the book.

By focusing on assessment of student understanding, Academy teachers learned to use their data to refine and guide instruction and support student progress toward unit learning goals. As one teacher stated,

> Many new curriculum projects are including "educative materials" (Davis & Krajcik, 2005) that assist the teacher with instruction and assessment. The notion is that materials for teachers can provide opportunities for teacher learning and serve as important resources for strengthening the quality of instruction. Features of such educative materials include, for example, suggestions for addressing students' persistent alternative conceptions, conceptual scoring guides that represent typical levels of understanding as students progress toward mastery of particular content, and follow-up instructional activities designed to address the range of student understanding.

[I have] made a total change in using assessments. . . . Formerly I used tests only as a summative tool. Now I use assessments as learning tools to capture student understanding and help me design my next instruction.

Another teacher, reflecting on one of her portfolios, commented,

Our assessment told us what kids don't get, and we now had to address what we're doing. We kept asking ourselves: "What is going on in our lessons? What are we teaching? Where are we supporting their learning?"

Academy teachers also learned that assessments are useful at every point during instruction. As one teacher reflected, "I have strengthened the way I use assessment information to guide instruction by planning ahead what formative assessments I was going to have." Teachers came to realize that pre-assessments provide more than a baseline measure; student responses on a pre-assessment guide unit planning when the tasks are designed to reveal what students understand. For a unit on mitosis, for example, a pre-assessment question might ask students what they know about cell division and body growth rather than ask what students know about mitosis. The teacher would then design a learning sequence that links the students' prior knowledge with the learning goals.

Teachers learned that the placement of juncture assessments at critical points in the development of conceptual understanding makes them particularly useful for instructional decisions. For example, when Del Vicer, an eighth-grade teacher, administered a juncture assessment of buoyancy and found that most of his students thought that "heavy" things sink in water, he was faced with a decision of how to address this alternative conception. He carefully chose activities in which the mass of the objects was the same but the volume of the objects was different. Students engaged in these activities were challenged to think about their original idea. Students continued to draw their ideas on a whiteboard and, through teacher questioning strategies, began to rethink their ideas. Something other than mass was making these objects sink! Through drawings and discussions, students began to recognize that the volume of the objects was different and that seemed to affect which item sank or floated in water. Del continued to add investigations based on additional information from assessment tasks. After these additional learning experiences, many of his students were able to construct a more scientifically accurate understanding of the mass/volume relationship in determining whether an object sinks or floats in water.

Academy teachers also learned that a sound assessment plan enables them to give students guidance in advance by establishing clear expectations for performance. These expectations, in turn, provide the basis for quality feedback. One teacher stated, "Defining and clarifying instructional goals before class became routine. . . . Sharing expectations with my students seemed to motivate them because they knew what I expected." When both teacher and student know what is expected, providing quality feedback to students can help improve student understanding (Black & Wiliam, 1998a, 1998b; National Research Council [NRC], 2001). Student feedback can be provided in a variety of ways, including sharing the rubrics before and after the work is done, emphasizing the particular qualities of responses that are needed to show more sophisticated understandings, and "move up" on the rubric (see Table 7.5 and Table 9.1), and having the whole class review a benchmark sample of quality work.

Assessment-centered teachers provide timely and relevant feedback to students, and they merge feedback and follow-up instruction, such as when teachers have students revisit their responses and then share and discuss their insights. As Academy teachers grew in their assessment expertise, some teachers began to anticipate their intended uses of assessment information by developing student-friendly criteria that served as the basis for feedback discussions with students. Others created multilevel criteria that incorporated recommendations for further learning experiences (see Connie McKenzie's rubric, Table 7.5, in Chapter 7).

The *ACT Portfolio* process of using assessment data to inform instruction promoted positive changes in teachers' instruction and assessment practices. Academy teachers shifted from an orientation focused on curriculum delivery and measurement of summative performance toward an appreciation of teaching for understanding and using assessment information to gauge student progress throughout instruction.

Two Sides of the Coin

Using evidence from student work to guide and revise instructional practice is only part of the equation for maximizing student understanding. Evidence from student work is also a critical resource for revising assessment tools, both tasks and scoring criteria, to capture student thinking more accurately. In tandem, refined assessments and instruction can lead to increases in student achievement. In Chapter 10, we consider how Academy teachers refined their assessments based on evidence from student work.

10

ACT Portfolio
Phase VII
Steps
1, 2, 3, 4

Use Evidence

Revise Assessments

In this chapter, we discuss how assessment-centered teachers use evidence from student work to refine or revise their assessment tools. We show how teachers analyze alignment of assessments to learning goals, sound content of the assessment items, range of student responses elicited by the assessment prompt, and clear expectations as the basis for assessment revision.

"Use Evidence to Revise Assessments" and the *Assessment-Centered Teaching Framework*

At this phase of the Assessment-Instruction Cycle, teachers have completed their analysis of the student work, revised their instruction, and provided students with feedback on their learning. They are now poised to evaluate and revise their assessment tools, and they begin by reviewing their understanding of Quality Tools—appropriate for use, fair, based on sound scientific concepts, and developmentally appropriate—from the Assessment

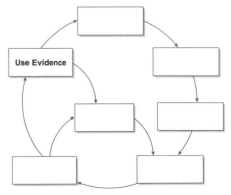

Knowledge Triangle. Using their knowledge of these assessment concepts, teachers judge whether adjustments need to be made to assessments to elicit the desired student responses and provide quality evidence of student progress toward the targeted learning goals. Knowledge of quality tools is critical if teachers are to modify assessment tasks and scoring criteria to create valid, fair, and reliable assessment tools.

Purpose of "Use Evidence to Revise Assessments"

There are two purposes for tool revision. First, a final review of assessments is a productive way for teachers to deepen their understanding of quality assessment tools to gauge student learning. Second, because many teachers will implement their units again in the future, the review helps them revise or refine their integrated instruction and assessment plan. Then teachers can add the revised tools to their archive of revised assessment and instructional strategies for the unit.

Role of "Use Evidence to Revise Assessments" in Building Reflective Practice

The assessment revision process includes the following four steps:

1. Match the assessment tool to the learning goals.
2. Evaluate the quality of the assessment tool.
3. Revise the assessment tool.
4. Administer the revised assessment tool and collect data.

1. Match Assessment Tool to the Learning Goals

To begin the revision process, teachers first examine assessment tools (tasks and scoring criteria) through the lens of their learning goals. Teachers select a tool for review and then ask themselves the following reflective questions:

- Where does this assessment appear in the Conceptual Flow?
- What evidence in the student work indicates how well the tool captures student understanding of the learning goal?
- What needs to be revised or refined to ensure that the task and scoring criteria assess the targeted concept(s)?
- To what extent did this assessment provide information on student understanding that helped guide my instruction? What needs to be revised to ensure that the assessment provides useful information?

In Chapter 9, we discussed how interpreting student work guided Carrie and her teaching partner, Juan, to change their instruction for *Properties of Matter* (National Science Resources Center, 2000) (Figures 9.1 and 9.2). They decided to restructure their conceptual flow to limit the number of concepts in the unit and emphasize the concept of density. They recognized that their changes in learning goals necessitated a revised assessment plan aligned with the new flow. They used the templates (described below) to revise their pre- and post-assessments, primarily deleting items that were no longer pertinent to the flow. They then selected several new juncture points that would provide information on their students' progression toward a complete understanding of density. They also determined which assessment items they had used previously might be used for these junctures.

2. Evaluate the Quality of the Assessment Tool

The second step in the process focuses teachers on examining the quality of the assessment tasks and scoring criteria. The tool can be evaluated by its alignment to the Quality Goals for Student Learning and Progress (Chapter 2) and its quality according to the concepts in the Assessment Knowledge Triangle. We illustrate four components of the evaluation process.

To what extent does the tool

1) align with learning goals (from step 1)?

2) contain sound content?

3) elicit a full range of student responses?

4) provide clear expectations for performance?

The *ACT Portfolio* provides two templates to guide the revision of assessment tools. The first is shown in Table 10.1. Using this template, teachers rate the quality of their tools against the four components listed above and then make decisions about which aspects of the tool are most critical to refine and improve.

Teachers often find that only certain aspects of a tool require revision or refinement. For example, a teacher may decide that the task elicits a full range of student responses but the scoring guide does not reflect that range. In that case, the teacher would refine only the scoring guide. On another occasion, a teacher might decide to revise a single item on an assessment. For example, a teacher might replace a multiple-choice item with a justified multiple-choice item (and scoring guide) to obtain more information on student thinking.

Using the *ACT Portfolio* prompts for this step, Carrie and Juan analyzed the multiple choice question shown in Figure 10.1. They concluded that the density item was aligned with the learning goals, had sound content, and was somewhat clearly written/drawn. However,

Table 10.1   Tool Rating Template

Component of Quality Tools	*Evaluate the* **Task** *To what extent does the* **task** *. . .*	*Evaluate the* **Criteria** *To what extent do the* **criteria** *. . .*
Alignment With Learning Goals	• Match instructional goals in the Conceptual Flow? *Not at all A bit Mostly*	• Match instructional goals in the Conceptual Flow? *Not at all A bit Mostly*
Scientifically Accurate Content	• Address scientifically accurate content? *Not at all A bit Mostly*	• Contain scientifically accurate content? *Not at all A bit Mostly*
Full Range of Student Responses	• Elicit the full range of conceptions in your classroom (all possible ESRs)? *Not at all A bit Mostly*	• Capture the full range of conceptions in your classroom (all possible ESRs)? *Not at all A bit Mostly*
Clear Expectations	• Communicate the purpose of the task? Provide clear and coherent directions? Use vocabulary appropriate for the grade level? *Not at all A bit Mostly*	• Communicate a quality response? Differentiate among levels of response? *Not at all A bit Mostly*

Figure 10.1 Building (Identifying) the Conceptual Flow

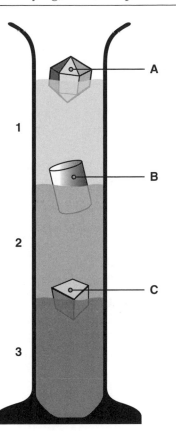

The graduated cylinder shown in the picture contains three liquids, labeled 1, 2, and 3. The objects (A, B, and C) in the cylinder are made from three different substances. Use the information in the picture to answer question A.

A. Which one of the following statements is correct?

    a. Object A is more dense than liquid 1.
    b. Object C is more dense than liquid 2.
    c. Object B is more dense than liquid 2.
    d. Object C is heavier than object B.

when Carrie and Juan analyzed their students' responses to this item (the correct answer is b), they found no clear-cut trend in student responses. The item did not elicit a full range of student responses and the teachers decided to revise the item so that student responses would provide evidence of alternative conceptions that could guide instruction. They also decided that they would need several items to assess student understanding of a concept as complex as relative density.

3. Revise the Assessment Tool

The third step in the process guides teachers to make specific revisions to the assessment tools based on their analysis in the prior two steps. Teachers use the expanded version of the template shown in Table 10.2.

The techniques outlined in the first row are useful if tasks or criteria are not well aligned with the targeted learning goals. For example, a teacher might eliminate unnecessary items that are not aligned with the learning goals, or if the task is well aligned to the learning goals but the criteria in the scoring guide are not, the teacher might use the techniques under "Quality of Criteria."

The second row of Table 10.2 concerns the accuracy of the science content of the assessment. Teachers can consult with others who have greater content knowledge or locate references to help them strengthen the scientific accuracy of the tasks and criteria.

The third row contains guidelines for strengthening tasks and criteria so that they capture the full range of student understanding. A teacher may use these guidelines, for example, to expand criteria to include the characteristics of a wider range of responses that are common for the grade level.

Carrie and Juan used the guidelines in the third row to revise their relative density multiple-choice question. They decided to modify the drawing so that it was evident that the three liquids were different from each other and that the objects were made of different materials. They decided to keep the shape of the objects different (as they were originally drawn) because they were interested in how students might respond to the shape, rather than to the density, of the object. They also added a follow-up question that asked students to explain their thinking for the answer they selected. By adding this prompt, the teachers expected to get a fuller range of student responses and hoped to identify students' alternative conceptions about density—for example, that heavy things sink or that larger sizes (volume) sink more than smaller sizes; the relationship of the density of the object to the density of the liquid; or the relationship of the density of the different liquids to each other.

Carrie and Juan also decided that they needed additional items to assess student understanding of relative density and its application in

Table 10.2 Revising the Assessment Tools

Component of Quality Tools	Quality of *Task* *How can this **task/item** be improved?*	Quality of *Criteria* *How can these **criteria** be improved?*
Alignment With Learning Goals	1. Match instructional goals more closely. • Review the section of the Conceptual Flow relevant to this task. • What were your learning goals? • Are they clear and measurable? • Revise the goals if necessary. • Examine task for fit with the Conceptual Flow. • Revise task to fit the Conceptual Flow more closely.	1. Match instructional goals more closely. • Review the section of the Conceptual Flow relevant to this task. • What were your learning goals? • Are they clear and measurable? • Revise the goals if necessary. • Examine criteria for fit with the Conceptual Flow • Revise criteria to include appropriate descriptors so they are aligned with your instructional goals and have the capacity to assess students' progress toward those goals.
Scientifically Accurate Content	2. Improve accuracy of scientific content. • Review task for accuracy of scientific content. Consult references or experts to help you. • Revise task accordingly.	2. Increase accuracy of scientific content. • Review criteria for accuracy of scientific content. Consult references or experts to help you. • Revise criteria accordingly.
Full Range of Student Responses	3. Improve the task so it provides evidence of the full range of student understandings and progress toward instructional goals. • Review your whole class Assessment Record for patterns and describe any patterns you find (e.g., a clustering at one end, a bell-shaped distribution). Is this pattern providing you with helpful information about student understanding?	3. Improve the criteria so they can provide evidence of the full range of student understandings and progress toward the instructional goals. • Review your whole class Assessment Record for patterns and describe any patterns you find (e.g., a clustering at one end, a bell-shaped distribution). Is this pattern providing you with helpful information about student understanding? A clustering at the high end, for example, may be meaningful

(Continued)

Table 10.2 (Continued)

Component of Quality Tools	Quality of **Task** *How can this **task/item** be improved?*	Quality of **Criteria** *How can these **criteria** be improved?*
	A clustering at the high end, for example, may be meaningful if you have been emphasizing this concept and you have other evidence that most students understand it. On the other hand, if this concept hasn't been emphasized in your instruction, then very high (or very low) performance many indicate a weakness in the task. • If the pattern raises any concerns, evaluate the quality of the task. Use guidelines elsewhere in this column to revise the task.	if you have been emphasizing this concept and you have other evidence that most students understand it. On the other hand, if this concept hasn't been emphasized in your instruction, then very high (or very low) performance may indicate a weakness in the criteria. • If the pattern raises any concerns, evaluate the quality of the criteria. Use guidelines elsewhere in this column to revise the criteria.
Clear Expectations	4. Improve the clarity of communication. Ensure that the purpose of the question, the content of the item, and the directions are clear. • Review administration guidelines, prompts, or setups to ensure that they communicate purpose of the task. You may need to review how you implemented the assessment as well as what is written. • Review the item for clarity (e.g., clear and coherent directions; appropriate vocabulary). • Review student work as evidence of students' understanding of the expectations and the task content. • Revise the directions or item content accordingly. Discuss any needed revisions in implementation of the assessment as well.	4. Improve the criteria so they more clearly communicate the characteristics of a "quality response." • Review the clarity of the criteria. • To what extent do the criteria clearly differentiate levels of response? • To what extent do the levels capture students' progress toward the instructional goals? • Revise criteria to show all levels of responses with specific examples. Rescore.

a new context. They consulted several assessment resources and selected an open-ended prompt that provided a list of phenomena (e.g., Earth's atmosphere, convection currents in magma, diatoms in ocean currents) and asked students to explain how density applied to each item.

4. Administer the Revised Assessment Tool and Collect Data

The fourth step in the assessment revision process is to gather data to determine if the assessment revisions have resulted in a higher-quality tool. Teachers may choose to administer the revised assessment as they are teaching the unit if feasible or administer it the next time they implement the unit. In either situation, assessment-centered teachers use student responses to inform and guide their instruction and to reflect on any further revisions that may be needed in the assessment tools. Thus the Assessment-Instruction Cycle continues to guide ongoing reflection.

Student work from the revised assessment used in the second round of teaching revealed how the students were thinking about density. Carrie and Juan noted that much of the class was still struggling with the alternative conception that heavy and/or large things sink. They decided to add several more student explorations where mass was held constant but the volume changed as well as where the mass varied but the volume was constant. Then they planned to assess the students again to see if students were better able to understand the mass-to-volume relationship.

Assessment Tool Revision Examples

The revisions that Carrie and Juan made in their task illustrate how one eighth-grade team used the Academy's tool revision templates. In this section, we present three additional examples to illustrate how assessment-centered teachers might use the tool revision process. The examples are from different grade levels and highlight different assessment revisions. The first revision strengthens alignment to learning goals and assessment of the full range of student responses, the second addresses sound content (i.e., the scientific accuracy of the tool), and the third addresses strengthening a rubric so it captures a range of student responses and provides clearer expectations for quality student work.

High School: Eliciting a Full Range of Student Responses

After administering a department-mandated comprehensive chemistry exam (multiple-choice, machine-scored), Ralph Alvados reviewed his assessment results. In many ways, he was satisfied with his students' performance; all students showed progress from pre- to post-assessment, and nearly all of his students met the department's competency scores for proficiency. In the past, he would have recorded scores, assigned grades, and considered the chemistry unit and the assessment complete. But as we shall see, when Ralph used the tool revision templates to evaluate the exam, he recognized its limitations.

Guided by the tool revision templates in Tables 10.1 and 10.2, Ralph first reviewed the unit's Conceptual Flow to check that his learning goals were aligned with the curriculum and the exam (Row #1 in Table 10.2). Satisfied with the alignment, he next turned to the prompts concerning elicitation of a full range of responses (Row #3 in Table 10.2).

Because he had reflected on the important learning goals of the unit, Ralph now recognized that the assessment provided limited information on student understanding of the important chemistry concepts—he could not identify students' alternative conceptions from their incorrect answers. Ralph realized that he needed a higher-quality assessment tool, but at this point, he hit a stumbling block. He couldn't change the department exam, nor did he think it would be fair to students to give them an additional assessment that would provide him with the information he was missing. He decided that he could ask students to explain their thinking on some of the key assessment items without changing the items themselves. To choose those items, Ralph consulted his Conceptual Flow again, then modified several traditional multiple-choice items to "justified" multiple-choice questions that required students to explain their answer. These items gave students the opportunity to demonstrate their understanding of key chemistry concepts in writing. To score these written responses, Ralph developed a four-point rubric that provided him with both qualitative and quantitative information on student understandings of key concepts using a Hybrid Assessment Record (Chapter 8).

From further review of whole class records for the pre and posttests, Ralph also realized that he needed better midpoint information on student learning. He consulted his Conceptual Flow and chose to develop a juncture assessment that focused on student understanding of the periodic table of elements, a critical component of his unit on chemical reactions. Table 10.3 contains the prompt for his newly devised juncture assessment. Notice that Ralph chose an open-ended prompt designed to reveal different levels of student understanding about the organization and use of the periodic table. By asking students to include examples, he could also analyze evidence of any confusion.

Through the tool revision protocol, Ralph strengthened the tools he used to measure student understanding.

Table 10.3 High School Chemistry Juncture Prompt

The periodic table has had an important impact on the field of chemistry. Please explain

1. how the periodic table is organized; and

2. how it is a useful tool for predicting chemical reactions.

Be sure to include examples and provide a complete explanation of your understanding. Write your response in an essay format.

Elementary School: Scientifically Accurate Content

Anna Rossa, a third-grade teacher, used the Academy templates to review tasks on a posttest her team developed for the *Earth Materials* (Full Option Science System [FOSS], 2001) unit. Using the templates, she learned that one of the tasks and its accompanying scoring guide were generating scientifically inaccurate conceptions.

The task was designed to assess the properties of rock and minerals, but when Anna reviewed student responses to this task, she noticed that more than half of her students used the attribute of color to determine if an object was a rock or a mineral. These students wrote that "all minerals were white." Curious about this pattern, she looked at the rock and mineral samples provided with the instructional materials and confirmed that all of the minerals in the kit were indeed white! Anna recognized that her students' responses to the assessment were based on their experiences with the materials in the kit, and she quipped that students had developed a "kit misconception." She immediately revised the kit by adding minerals of various colors, and she added an item to the assessment that asked students if color is a possible way to identify minerals. Anna's insight about "kit misconceptions" shows how a teacher's careful interpretation of patterns in student responses can identify weaknesses in the scientific accuracy of the instructional materials, assessment tasks, and criteria.

Elementary School: Refining Criteria

Our final example returns us to the 5-point rubric that Connie McKenzie developed to document student progress towards learning goals in *Earth Materials* (FOSS, 2001). Her original scoring guide, illustrated in Table 7.5 and shown again in Table 10.4, contained detailed information about what students needed to learn or to do to move to the next level of understanding, and Connie used this tool to assess student learning throughout the unit. She monitored student progress by generating Assessment Records of her students' performance on a series of assessments. But as useful as this guide was, when Connie used the tool revision templates to evaluate the guide, she discovered that it needed refinement.

At the conclusion of the unit, Connie reviewed student work and noticed that responses scored as Rock Expert contained more information about student thinking than her rubric captured. Her criteria needed to be refined to include a fuller range of student responses, and Connie felt that the revision would also communicate clearer expectations to her students. Compare the "Need to Learn" column in Table 10.4 with the same column in Table 10.5. Notice that Connie has incorporated the science thinking processes (observation, comparison, cause and effect, application) as part of the rubric design. She has also incorporated the notion that students can go beyond the Rock Expert level of understanding, an important aspect to working with students who enter a class with a significant background of knowledge and experience.

Table 10.4   Connie's Rubric: Refining Criteria

Level	What the Student Already Knows	Expected Student Response	What the Student Needs to Learn
RE	**Rock Expert** Student knows that the property of hardness can be used to classify minerals and that a harder mineral always scratches a softer mineral.	Student agrees that rubbing two materials together is a legitimate test for hardness. States that a harder mineral will always scratch a softer mineral. Concludes that because gray mineral was scratched, the whiter mineral is harder.	
RN	**Rock Novice** Student knows that the property of hardness can be used to classify minerals.	Student agrees that rubbing two materials together is a legitimate test for hardness. States that a harder mineral will always scratch a softer mineral.	Student needs to understand that because the whiter mineral is scratched, the gray mineral must be harder than the whiter mineral.
RO	**Rock Observer** Student knows that when two rocks are rubbed together, one will scratch the other, but can't identify hardness as a cause for the scratch.	Student agrees that rubbing two materials together is a legitimate test for hardness.	Student needs to understand that the scratch test is a way to identify rock hardness.
UF	**Unconventional Feature** Student writes that one rock scratched the other because it was bigger. Student thinks size of the rock determines its hardness.	Student gives some information about the minerals or the hardness that does not pertain to the task or includes an alternative conception (e.g., size = hardness).	Student needs to observe that rocks can cause scratches on one another and that size is not a factor in the hardness of a rock.

Table 10.5   Connie's Rubric Refined: Changes in Italics

Level	What the Student Already Knows	Expected Student Response	What the Student Needs to Learn
RE	**Rock Expert** Student knows that the property of hardness can be used to classify minerals and that a harder mineral always scratches a softer mineral.	Student agrees that rubbing two materials together is a legitimate test for hardness. States that a harder mineral will always scratch a softer mineral. Concludes that because gray mineral was scratched, the whiter mineral is harder.	*Student needs to be able to apply the knowledge to new situations with more than two minerals.*
RN	**Rock Novice** Student knows that the property of hardness can be used to classify minerals.	Student agrees that rubbing two materials together is a legitimate test for hardness. States that a harder mineral will always scratch a softer mineral.	Student needs to understand *a cause-and-effect line of reasoning:* if the white mineral is scratched, then the gray mineral must be harder than the white mineral.
RO	**Rock Observer** Student knows that when two rocks are rubbed together, one will scratch the other, but can't identify hardness as a cause for the scratch.	Student agrees that rubbing two materials together is a legitimate test for hardness.	Student needs to understand that the scratch test is a way to identify rock hardness by *comparing which material scratches which material.*
UF	**Unconventional Feature** Student writes that one rock scratched the other because it was bigger. Student thinks size of the rock determines its hardness.	Student gives some information about the minerals or the hardness that does not pertain to the task or includes an alternative conception (e.g., size = hardness).	Student needs to *observe* that rocks can cause scratches on one another and that size is not a factor in the hardness of a rock.

"Use Evidence to Revise Assessments" and Teacher Change

Assessment tool revision is an important experience in the *ACT Portfolio* process. As teachers evaluate and revise assessment tasks and criteria, they consolidate what they have learned about quality tools. For many, the process expanded their thinking.

> *Going through the process: conceptual flow—>assessment tool (pre-, juncture, post-)—>student work—>refining instruction and/or assessment has been a mind opener! We struggle with assessment and instruction, but now I have a process to make the improvements that help my students learn!*

The revision process promoted a confident and more reflective stance toward assessments that teachers carried with them after the Academy.

> *[Revision] is the area in which I have seen the most growth in my understanding. The intricate questioning and analysis has forced me to evaluate the assessment tools and caused me to come to radical changes—for instance, throwing out an assessment and starting over to make one more appropriate.*

> *I have been much more confident and "skilled" when I look at any type of assessment tool. I am not an expert yet, but I have been able to truly express my own "review" of various assessment tools.*

Each of the tool revision guidelines—each row in Table 10.2—contributed to teacher learning. For example, Academy teachers came to value the importance of strengthening the alignment of their assessment tools with the learning goals in their Conceptual Flow (Row # 1). One teacher reflected, "I have learned to continuously evaluate my tools with respect to my Concept Flow." Another realized that "developer-created assessments must be checked and analyzed to determine if their questions are assessing the same objectives you are looking for." One middle school teacher was very clear about her learning:

I have learned from looking at my assessments to see if they're actually testing what I want my kids to understand. I've been teaching about mass, I've been teaching about volume, I've been teaching about density—but what I really need to know is do they know how to apply mass and volume to get density? And, are my assessments actually looking at that?

Teachers also learned from using Row #3 of Table 10.2 to improve tools so that they provided evidence of the full range of student understandings and progress. For many teachers, the *ACT Portfolio* process of using student work as a resource for assessment refinement was totally new.

Prior to CAESL, I just made a rather subjective decision as to the value and quality of an assessment without much analysis. The Academy and the portfolio helped me learn to qualify and quantify my decisions based on student responses.

Using the tool revision templates, teachers learned a detailed process for revising tools to better capture student understanding.

The tools I used were not initially very reliable and/or accurate, or at least I found I did not get the results I anticipated. However, going through this process has allowed me the opportunity to adjust and match what students need, and I have gained insight into how to adjust my assessment tools to better understand the students' learning.

As we discussed in Chapter 9, Academy teachers were learning to use student work to improve their *instruction,* and as we have just shown, teachers were also learning to use student work to improve their *assessment.* Working through all phases of the Assessment-Instruction Cycle helped to shift many teachers from teacher-centered to student-centered practice. One teacher commented on this shift with openness and honesty regarding her classroom practice: "Now I don't blame the students for the result—I look at the assessment tool, and, of course, my instruction."

Changing Practice Through Collaboration

The Academy provided time and space for teachers to work together on assessment and instruction, and teachers greatly appreciated the collaboration. We received comments such as "Providing a collaborative forum to get input from other teachers has been invaluable," "The table talk about the whole process has been very important for my development," and "The Academy has been a good opportunity to interact with colleagues about creating assessments that really measure what students understand."

Building a learning community through collaboration was a major goal of our professional development. Many structures and strategies supported the development of this goal. In Chapters 11 and 12, we describe the Academy and our rationale for the choices we made in designing a professional development program that had transformative impact on teachers' assessment practice.

11

Professional Development Design

In this chapter, we discuss our professional development design and share some of the challenges and decisions that we made during the course of the Center for the Assessment and Evaluation of Student Learning (CAESL) professional development program. We invite you to learn from our experience and adapt what is relevant and useful to your context.

This is the story of the CAESL professional development program known as the Science Assessment Leadership Academy. In this chapter, we describe our goals, the process we used to develop the plan for the Academy, and some of the challenges we encountered in designing the Academy's tools and strategies. We outline our design process in detail to illustrate the many considerations and decisions that were made as we undertook the task of building teacher and district capacity for quality assessment practices in science. The purpose in sharing this account is to support others (e.g., staff developers and teacher educators) as they consider how to design programs to support Assessment-Centered Teaching. We do not envision that our program will be replicated exactly, but we believe that the Academy principles and strategies can be adapted for other professional development settings and will provide a useful resource for future work with teachers and districts.

Background

In 2000, the National Science Foundation (NSF) funded the Centers for Learning and Teaching (CLT) as part of its national systemic reform programs. These centers were intended to be comprehensive, research-based efforts that addressed critical issues and national needs of the science, technology, engineering, and mathematics instructional workforce across the spectrum of formal and informal education. The CLT's goals included a systemic approach to the development and enhancement of the instructional workforce (kindergarten through graduate school) in an environment of research and practice. The Center for the Assessment and Evaluation of Student Learning was conceived and funded (2001–2006) as one of the CLT centers. CAESL was a collaboration of four institutions: WestEd; University of California, Los Angeles; University of California, Berkeley, Graduate School of Education and Lawrence Hall of Science; and Stanford University.

The Center's mission was to strengthen the quality of assessment at all levels of the educational system and to ensure coherence for the program. CAESL focused specifically on supporting high-quality assessment in science. The Center's goals were organized into five strands: 1) increase the number of graduate students in assessment fields, 2) enhance current teacher practice and district policies around assessment through professional development, 3) initiate assessment courses for preservice education, 4) conduct research on classroom assessment, and 5) create tools for public understanding of assessment. The goal of the Science Assessment Leadership Academy was focused on the second strand—to enhance current teacher practice and district policies around assessment through professional development—and the Academy also served as a focus for Strand 4 research on how teachers learn about and implement classroom assessment.

Using the *Professional Development Design Framework*

In planning for the CAESL professional development program, we drew upon the *Professional Development Design Framework* (Loucks-Horsley, Love, Stiles, Mundry, & Hewson, 2003) for science and mathematics education. A graphic representation of the model is displayed in Figure 11.1. At the center of the framework, illustrated in the rectangles connected with horizontal arrows, is a planning sequence incorporating the following: committing to a vision and a set of standards, analyzing student learning and other data, goal setting, planning, doing, and evaluating. The circles above and below the planning sequence represent important inputs to the design process that can help professional developers make informed decisions. These inputs cue designers to consider the extensive bases of knowledge and belief that can inform their work, to understand the unique features of their context, to draw on a wide repertoire of professional development strategies, and to wrestle with critical issues that mathematics and science education reformers will encounter, regardless of their contexts (Loucks-Horsley et al, 2003, pp. 3–4).

We used this framework as the authors intended, as "an ideal to strive toward, rather than an accurate depiction of how it always happens or a lockstep prescription for how it should" (p. 5). In the sections below, we discuss how we used each input component of the framework (i.e., the circles) to guide program design and implementation (i.e., the rectangles) of the Science Assessment Leadership Academy. A note of caution: the framework looks linear and sequential, but it really isn't. What is most important is to pay attention to the inputs—where they impact the design of the program and how they are addressed as implementation occurs. We share our context first because we believe it helps frame our story. In reality, we began with our knowledge and beliefs as we envisioned the program.

Figure 11.1   Professional Development Framework

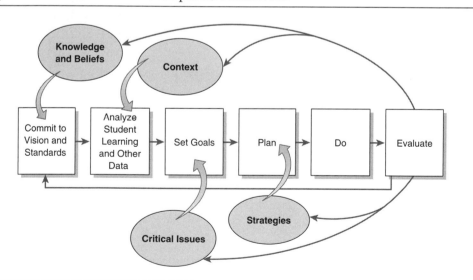

Design Framework for Professional Development in Science and Mathematics, Loucks-Horsley, Love, Stiles, Mundry, and Hewson, 2003. Corwin Press. Reprinted with permission.

Context Factors

Context refers to the circumstances or events that form the environment within which the professional development takes place. Loucks-Horsley et al. (2003) direct professional developers to "define and assess their current reality" (p. 54) in the following contextual categories as they plan a program: information about student learning, teacher learning, organizational structures and leadership, policies, resources, history of professional development, and parents and community. Four of these categories were most pertinent to our work: policies, history of professional development, teacher learning, and organizational structures. The two middle categories are combined in the following discussion.

Existing policies. In the early 2000s, assessment was a heated topic of debate in many arenas of educational and public discourse. It still is. Science teachers and administrators were concerned that the goals of large-scale testing often conflicted with the goals of classroom assessment. Testing, not teaching, seemed to be the preoccupation of many districts. Classroom assessment often did not match state assessments in format or content. State testing provided educators with limited information to guide teaching and learning. At best, teachers received annual information on the performance of last year's students, and sometimes they received data less frequently than that. Many testing programs—especially in science—neglected certain grade levels (e.g., California administers science tests only at Grades five, eight, and ten) or ignored specific content (e.g., California has no science on the high school exit exam). CAESL's mission was to strengthen assessment at all levels of the educational system, and it was clear that for science, there were many gaps and imbalances. Our goal was to address at least one component of the system—classroom assessment—and to provide the infrastructure for leadership development that could influence the rest of the system. We set out to design an intensive program to build science teachers' capacities to make classroom assessment central to learning. We took on a worthy challenge amid the pressures of high-stakes tests that focused particularly on student reading and mathematics scores.

Professional development and teacher learning. Professional development focused on science assessment was still rare in California districts, despite a strong research base advocating quality assessment in the classroom. Building on documents like the National Research Council's (NRC) *National Science Education Standards* (1996) and *Classroom Assessment and the National Science Education Standards* (2001), we envisioned a professional development program that would bring together teachers and administrators in district teams with the long-term goal of developing a balanced and systemic science assessment program for their districts. We wanted to break the trend of district assessment departments having little relationship with curriculum and instruction departments other than to give them the "bad news" data.

We also wanted district teams to be familiar enough with quality assessment practices that they could recognize the misuse of assessment data. For example, they should be able to recognize the (often reactionary) tendency to establish quick-fix professional development programs that address needs that may or may not be supported by data. We wanted a professional development program that resulted in teachers and districts proactively and thoughtfully changing their assessment practices.

Organizational structures. CAESL was an organization created to foster collaboration among diverse professionals, and we decided that our work would be strengthened if we invited CAESL educational researchers to collaborate with us in the design of the Academy program and our conceptual framework. We wanted our program to be research based and to bridge the chasm that often divides research and practice. The collaboration was an exercise in building a new kind of learning community of diverse professionals working with very different theories of action to improve science education. Over a period of two years, we worked side by side to plan, implement, evaluate, and revise the evolving Academy design. Along the way, participating teachers and administrators also provided input to the program. As a result, our design was significantly modified as the program unfolded based on the views and experiences of all its stakeholders.

In addition to these four context factors that directly informed our professional development design, we also considered important context factors for the participating districts. Data about student learning in science was sparse and often limited by the type of assessment and its administration (e.g., in California. only fifth, eighth, and tenth graders are tested by the state for science, and only 10 percent of that assessment addresses investigation and experimentation). While many California districts had a history of science professional development for teachers, most of those programs focused on content and pedagogy, not assessment. Similarly, existing leadership professional development programs focused on leading curriculum efforts but not assessment. These district context factors helped inform our goal to create a professional development program that would place science assessment "front and center."

Knowledge and Beliefs

Loucks-Horsley et al. (2003) address the knowledge base for professional development as a combination of knowledge and beliefs.

> Knowledge refers to information that is sure, solid, dependable and supported by research. Beliefs are what we think we know (Ball, 1996) or may be coming to know based on new information. They are supported by experience and people are strongly committed to them. (p. 31)

The *Professional Development Design Framework* guides professional developers to examine their ideas about teaching and learning, as well as professional development and teacher change, when planning their programs. Through our reflections and discussions, we found that our knowledge and beliefs were grounded in 1) change theory, 2) inquiry-based instruction, 3) teaching and learning cycles, 4) the interdependence of instruction and assessment, 5) professional learning communities, and 6) principles of effective professional development. We used these core beliefs and knowledge to formalize our vision and to inform our planning and selection of strategies.

Change theory. We began the project with the stance that change is possible. Despite all the pressures of the educational system (time, student demographics, district and state policies), we believe it *is* possible for educators to integrate and implement quality curriculum, instruction, *and* assessment. Teachers are professionals who care deeply about the learning of all students, and they are committed to finding ways to strengthen their practices to support student progress. They can rarely do it alone, however, and professional learning communities are almost always essential vehicles for changing teacher practice and school culture. Teachers also need authentic opportunities for learning practices that have immediate value for their students and their contexts. Therefore, we decided that workshops and activities around assessment should have a strong connection to the curriculum being taught. With this in mind, we engaged teachers in authentic tasks, like those in the *ACT Portfolio,* to provide rich, job-embedded professional development opportunities and to respect the use of teachers' valuable time.

Inquiry-based instruction. Foundational to our work in science professional development (as well as curriculum development) is inquiry-based science education as defined in the *National Science Education Standards* (NRC, 1996):

Scientific inquiry refers to the diverse ways in which scientists study the natural world and propose explanations based on the evidence derived from their work. Inquiry also refers to the activities of students in which they develop knowledge and understanding of scientific ideas, as well as an understanding of how scientists study the natural world. (p. 23)

For the most part, the science instructional materials used in the program exemplified inquiry-based approaches to teaching science. We also concur with the educational research that has documented the critical need for students to actively build new knowledge based on their prior understandings, as summarized in *How People Learn* (Bransford, Brown, & Cocking, 1999). This knowledge and belief about teaching and learning were made explicit in our approach to using assessment tools to probe for deep understanding of science concepts. (See Chapter 7, "Analyze: Interpret Student Work Using Scoring Criteria.")

Teaching and learning cycles. The professional development team also had the core belief that assessment should be viewed as a component of effective teaching, *not* as a wholly separate domain of professional expertise. Both effective instruction and assessment begin with the establishment of clear learning goals (Wiggins & McTighe, 2005), followed by a process of backward mapping to the design of instruction and assessment. To teach for understanding, teachers must employ formative assessment that provides them with accurate information about student learning and progress toward those goals. Both instruction and formative assessment must be guided by research on conceptual development (Driver, Squires, Rushworth, & Wood-Robinson, 1994; Kennedy, Brown, Draney, & Wilson, 2005) to ensure that the established goals are feasible and developmentally appropriate. Finally, both instruction and assessment must be continually refined through cycles of teaching and assessment of learning (Bybee, 1997). The connections between these features of assessment and instruction are represented in the phases of the Assessment-Instruction Cycle (see Chapter 2, Figure 2.4) and are the result of our strong belief in the need to weave together assessment and instruction.

Interdependence of instruction and assessment. While assessment cannot be isolated from teaching practice, we recognize that assessment expertise does require certain specialized concepts and technical skills. Through the CAESL collaboration, we had access to assessment theory and research (e.g., Black & Wiliam, 1998a, 1998b; NRC,

2001; Stiggins, 2002) as well as personal consultation with the CAESL research team of assessment experts, Joan Herman (CRESST at UCLA), Richard Shavelson (Stanford), and Mark Wilson (UC Berkeley). With these resources as our foundation, we identified the assessment knowledge and beliefs that are represented in the *Assessment-Centered Teaching Framework* (see Chapter 2). Readers will recall that the vertices of the Assessment Knowledge Triangle are "Quality Goals for Student Learning and Progress," "Quality Tools," and "Quality Use." This knowledge concerning the technical aspects and use of assessment tools formed the basis of the various presentations, group discussions, and individual reflections experienced by participants throughout the Academy.

Professional learning communities and teacher leadership. The tools and processes for Assessment-Centered Teaching described in Chapters 4–10 are also based on work in the field surrounding professional learning communities and building high-performing cultures and teacher leadership. We found that our work resonated with the findings of Craig et al. (2005) of continuously improving schools, where high-performing schools pay attention to the learning culture, involvement of all stakeholders, effective teaching, shared leadership, shared goals for learning, and purposeful student assessment (p. 6). Our professional development activities were designed based on a respect for the range of experience and expertise that teachers brought to the project. We engaged teachers in a joint reflective process that required them to share responsibilities with us as they worked toward implementation of quality assessment practices in their classrooms. We also supported and acknowledged their contributions as emerging assessment leaders in their districts. We felt that to build capacity for science assessment within and across districts, we needed to support the growth of professional communities invested in making the system work.

Principles of effective professional development and requirements for transformative learning experiences. Finally, we built our program based on acknowledged principles of effective professional development (Loucks-Horsley et al., 2003, p. 44) and the requirements for transformative learning experiences (Thompson & Zeuli, 1999, pp. 355–357). All activities were driven by a well-defined image of effective classroom learning and teaching, and we provided multiple opportunities for teachers to build their content and pedagogical content knowledge and examine their practices. The learning experiences created high levels of cognitive dissonance to "upset the balance" between the teachers' beliefs and practices and new information about assessment and instruction, and they provided time and support for the teachers to think through the dissonance they experienced. The ideas represented and techniques used for quality assessment were research based and engaged teachers as adult learners in developing new repertoires of teaching and assessment practice for use with their students. We provided extensive opportunities for teachers to collaborate with colleagues and other experts to improve their practice, and we supported participants in new leadership roles for assessment. These principles particularly impacted the strategies used in the Academy sessions and are discussed in more detail below in the section entitled "Strategies for Professional Development."

Critical Issues

We took seriously Loucks-Horsley et al.'s (2003) repeated warning about addressing critical issues in professional development. Issues mentioned as "critical to the success of programs everywhere, regardless of context" include time for professional development, equity and diversity, professional culture, leadership, capacity building for sustainability, scaling up, and garnering public support (p. 9). The idea is that prior consideration of these factors can help professional developers avoid commonly encountered pitfalls and can help to ensure success of the program, or "ignore these [critical issues] at your own peril" (p. 79). Our program focused on addressing four critical issues: (1) time for professional development, (2) ensuring equity, (3) building professional culture, and (4) developing leadership.

Time for professional development. Quality assessment and thoughtful reflection about teaching and learning take a significant amount of time. We sought to leverage prior professional development efforts by recruiting five district teams who valued this approach and had previously actively participated in other long-term, in-depth professional development programs. To ensure that Academy teams devoted sufficient time, we asked them to make a three-year commitment (the last two years are addressed in this book) to our program, which included statewide Academy meetings and on-site work. Participants devoted approximately three weeks per year to structured Academy activities as well as considerable individual time implementing and analyzing classroom assessments.

Ensuring equity. Loucks-Horsley et al. (2003) suggest three guiding questions for ensuring equity:

1. Is access to the professional development experience equitable?

2. Does the design of the professional development invite full engagement and learning by participants?

3. Does the content of the professional development experience include the issues of equitable opportunity for all students to learn science . . . and participate in careers in science . . . ? (p. 86)

Our consideration of these issues was made doubly important by our Academy focus on assessment tools and uses that are fair and equitable. Therefore, we gave much consideration to these issues in developing our goals, design, and program strategies.

California is a state with great diversity in student population and school characteristics, and we wanted to represent that diversity in the Academy. When we considered which districts to invite, we created a matrix of characteristics that represented the diverse needs in our state. These included student demographics (ethnicity, socioeconomic background, language), school size and geography (urban, suburban, rural), and school level (elementary, middle, and high school). We also requested that participating districts form teams whose members were representative of their teacher and student populations.

To meet the needs of diverse adult learners, our professional development sessions were organized in a variety of formats, including large groups, small groups, and individual work. We provided a range of resources and implemented a variety of instructional strategies to increase teachers' assessment knowledge and provided multiple opportunities in which to apply their learning. To meet the diverse needs of California science students, our *ACT Portfolio* prompts emphasized assessment tools and processes that are fair and unbiased for *all* students. Yvette's story (Chapter 1) illustrates the impact of the equity focus on one Academy teacher's efforts to improve teaching and learning for all students.

Building a professional culture. Strong professional cultures are essential to changing norms of practice and pedagogy (McLaughlin & Talbert, 2001). Transforming teacher practices is complex and requires a community of professionals working together to shift their thinking. Therefore, building a professional culture of thoughtful reflection about assessment was a core aspect of our work, and respect and collaboration were key expectations emphasized in our group dynamic.

Because learners at any age need time for individual reflection as well as collaboration, our Academy design balanced opportunities for collaboration with individual reflection. We implemented a portfolio strategy that enabled teachers to build on the assessment knowledge and skills they brought to the process and that provided opportunities for them to acquire new knowledge and skills working with others as well as on their own.

Our professional culture around quality assessment practices was supported by the structure of our Academy program. We created an Academy that built interdependence and support within and across districts (see Figure 11.2). The Academy consisted of five district-based teams of teachers from several K–12 grade levels and an administrator. At statewide meetings, all district teams attended common learning sessions, resulting in lively cross-district and cross-grade-level discussions. Teachers were also assigned to cross-district grade-level teams who taught the same instructional units. Together these teachers planned assessments and reflected on student work from common instructional materials. In meetings in their home districts, Academy participants shared what they were learning with colleagues

Figure 11.2 Building Interdependence

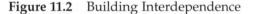

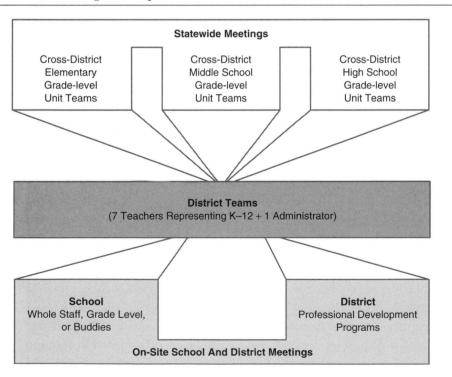

who had not attended the Academy. In these ways, assessment ideas and resources were "cross-fertilized" between schools and districts throughout the CAESL experience. The Academy's approach to reflective practice built a professional culture of lifelong learning and appreciation for the benefits of collaboration.

Developing leadership. Our original goal was to establish and support district leadership teams that could eventually lead district-wide improvement in science assessment. However, because the needs, opportunities, and circumstances of each district were so varied, our district teams took on varied roles and approaches to leadership. We shifted our emphasis from districtwide leadership to leadership within the district/school (e.g., with colleagues, at grade-level or department-wide meetings, via schoolwide professional development or selected district professional development programs). Each team came to define leadership as "taking responsibility for something you care about."

With both theoretical and practical knowledge of Assessment-Centered Teaching, Academy participants could lead by example or share what they had learned through professional development programs with a variety of audiences. For example, one district leadership team introduced the Conceptual Flow and RAIM in districtwide teacher institutes. Another team established study groups with their grade-level colleagues for analyzing student work from common instructional units. Still another team assisted their district in developing district benchmark assessments for monitoring student progress toward key learning goals in science. We encouraged flexible leadership roles so that teams and individual teachers could meet the needs of their particular contexts, and we provided support for the choices they made about influencing broader assessment efforts within their schools and districts.

Strategies

Strategies, as depicted in the *Professional Development Design Framework,* refer to proven methods for professional learning. Loucks-Horsley et al. (2003) describe 18 different teacher learning strategies that are considered "robust examples of professional development in mathematics and science and are consistent with the principles of effective professional development" (p. 11). Our design combined several of these well-tested strategies as well as some new strategies (e.g., the *ACT Portfolio*) in unique ways to form our plan of action—the Academy. The Academy served as our primary "vehicle," or structure, in which professional development was provided. We first discuss the structure of the Academy and the nature of the activities and then discuss the specific strategies we selected to meet our program goals.

Academy structure. The Science Assessment Leadership Academy was originally intended to develop a new set of district teams each year who were knowledgeable about quality assessment practices and who had the efficacy to influence science assessment in their school districts. As the program evolved, and to build upon the strengths of the entire CAESL program and our participants, we decided to concentrate our efforts on building the five original district teams' knowledge and skills regarding classroom assessment and instructional practices. Each of the five district teams then took up the charge of disseminating quality assessment practices to district colleagues in the manner they felt was appropriate for their context.

As noted earlier, our long-term work with the five districts was organized as a year-round program that consisted of statewide meetings alternating with on-site implementation. Statewide meetings were scheduled as five-day institutes in the summer and 2 three-day seminars during the school year. On-site implementation sessions were conducted in classrooms as well as in meetings at school or district sites. In total, teams participated in Academy activities for 21 days in each year of the CAESL professional development program.

Nature of academy activities. We offered a wide range of opportunities for collaboration on authentic tasks over the two-year period described in this book. During statewide meetings (indicated as rectangles in Figure 11.3), all participants worked together in activities designed to build knowledge of methods for developing quality goals for student learning and progress, quality assessment tools, and quality uses of assessments. Then, in grade-level teams, teachers applied these methods to their inquiry-based instructional units as they planned the assessments for the unit. Teachers returned to their classrooms to implement their units, gather student work from assessments throughout the unit, analyze the student work, and used the evidence to guide instruction and provided feedback to students.

When the teams convened at the next statewide meeting, grade-level teams compared and evaluated the ways they had interpreted student work and modified instruction and/or assessments. Most unit-alike teams had the opportunity to plan, implement, and revise their unit assessment plan twice (Fall 2003 and Fall 2004) and found that process a powerful learning opportunity.

During on-site sessions (indicated as ovals in Figure 11.3), district teams met to strategize how to disseminate learning to colleagues or, in some cases, to assist in the planning of districtwide science assessments. At school sites, teachers taught in their classrooms and used common preparation time and afterschool meetings to share their

Figure 11.3 Academy Cycle

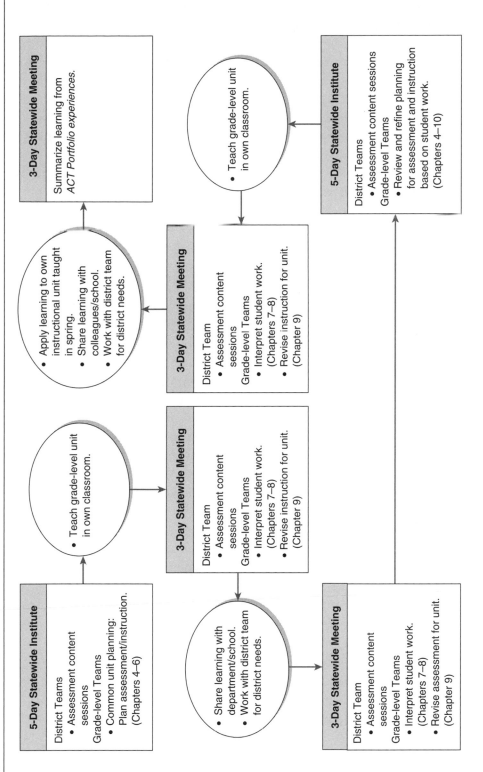

growing assessment expertise and collaborate with colleagues who did not attend the Academy program.

Specific strategies. Several core strategies provided significant opportunities for teachers to build their assessment knowledge and apply their emerging understandings as they implemented effective teaching and assessment approaches with students, including the *Assessment-Centered Teaching Portfolio,* curriculum replacement units, and developing leadership. Each of these core strategies incorporated a variety of activities to develop participants' knowledge and skills.

The ACT Portfolio. The *ACT Portfolio* process (see Chapters 4–10) was our core strategy for supporting Assessment-Centered Teaching. We were encouraged by the success of the portfolio process used by the National Board of Professional Teaching Standards (2001) and were hopeful that teachers could similarly build knowledge and strengthen their teaching and assessment practices through both collaborative and independent reflection as supported by the *ACT Portfolio.* As described throughout this book, the portfolio guided teachers through a process of planning, analysis, implementation, and evaluation of assessments for specific science units. Many teachers completed two or three portfolios over two years, and the opportunity to revise their earlier portfolios turned out to be a particularly valuable experience. The teachers' commitment to continued improvement was evidence that the *ACT Portfolio* process can support a lifelong commitment to improving student learning.

Through Academy activities, teachers built the necessary assessment knowledge to complete the portfolio. For example, to increase knowledge of quality assessment tools, teachers engaged in study groups and read about the technical aspects for ensuring that assessments are fair and unbiased, valid for their intended purpose, reliable, and addressing developmentally sound content. To understand better the development and revision of scoring criteria, teachers analyzed a variety of scoring tools (scoring guides/rubrics) and compared their usefulness in characterizing student understanding. To master tools for uncovering student thinking, teachers participated in facilitated learning sessions that demonstrated strategies for increasing student-to-student conversations and scientific discourse.

Curriculum replacement units. Because one of our goals was to integrate assessment throughout instructional planning and implementation, we selected a strategy that would keep teachers' instructional materials at the center of the work. Curriculum replacement units are specific instructional materials, or units, that are meant to replace one part of a teacher's regular science curriculum but not the entire curriculum. We selected inquiry-based science units (Table 11.1) because they exemplify the best practices in teaching and assessment that we were advocating and provide opportunities for students to engage in learning science through inquiry. Many of these inquiry units were developed with the support of the National Science Foundation and utilize research-based instructional strategies that had been field tested with students prior to publication.

Table 11.1   Examples of Inquiry-Based Instructional Materials Used in the Academy

Grade Span	Curriculum Developer	Title
Primary	Lawrence Hall of Science, Full Option Science System (FOSS)	Solids and Liquids
Upper Elementary	Lawrence Hall of Science, Full Option Science System (FOSS)	Earth Materials
6th Grade	Lawrence Hall of Science, Great Explorations in Math and Science (GEMS)xt	Plate Tectonics: The Way The Earth Works, Convection: A Current Event
7th Grade	Science Education for Public Understanding Project (SEPUP)	Science and Life Issues
7th Grade	National Science Resources Center, Science and Technology Concepts for Middle School (STC/MS)	Organisms— Macro to Micro
8th Grade	National Science Resources Center, Science and Technology Concepts for Middle School (STC/MS)	Properties of Matter
High School Biology	Biological Science Curriculum Study (BSCS)	Biology: A Human Approach
High School Chemistry	American Chemical Society (ACS)	Chemistry in the Community (Chem Com)

In addition to working with inquiry units recommended through the Academy, teachers also applied what they were learning to the assessments provided in their district's adopted instructional materials, materials that were not necessarily inquiry-based. It was important to the participants—and to us—to learn how Assessment-Centered Teaching can be designed and implemented for different kinds of instructional materials.

Leadership. As noted in the section on developing leadership, building district capacity was a major goal of the Academy. Our approach to accomplishing this goal was to provide knowledge and skill sets around assessment, leadership, and professional development. The curriculum for leadership included change theory, working with adults, temperament and leadership styles, facilitating teams, and using tools such as the Concerns-Based Adoption Model (CBAM) for designing professional development.

We provided opportunities and technical assistance for participants to work on authentic tasks that involved implementation of their knowledge of assessment and professional development and their leadership skills. Some worked on large-scale projects (e.g., incorporating their CAESL knowledge into existing districtwide summer institutes), while others worked schoolwide or at grade levels. All Academy teachers worked with a "buddy" in the second year to share the *ACT Portfolio* process and distill it so it could become part of regular assessment planning and practice at the school site.

At statewide Academy meetings, we provided the opportunity for districts to discuss how they were envisioning and enacting their plan to disseminate the principles and strategies from the *ACT Framework*. The professional learning community aspect of the program helped to encourage participants to work together to share ideas and solve emerging issues in leadership and implementation.

A Return to the *Professional Development Design Framework*

As stated at the beginning of this chapter, we used the *Professional Development Design Framework* as "an ideal to strive toward." Reflecting on the inputs of knowledge and beliefs, context, critical issues, and strategies helped us focus on our vision and goals. As a result of considering these inputs, we were strategic and thoughtful about our plan of action. The structured Academy activities enabled teachers to grow and deepen their understanding of assessment. Providing an infrastructure for leadership activities and supporting flexible roles for all participants encouraged broader dissemination of Assessment-Centered Teaching principles.

Throughout the project, we continuously collected data from the *ACT Portfolios,* teacher interviews, and questionnaires to evaluate and improve our program. We actively revisited our beliefs about teacher learning and frequently checked our strategies against the changing context of the districts. While our core strategies remained foundational, we redesigned many Academy sessions to meet the emerging needs of the participants. As a community of learners—teachers, professional developers, and researchers—we engaged in our own cycle of continuous improvement. We share some of that learning in Chapter 12.

12

Reflective Practice for Transformative Learning

Lessons Learned

In this chapter, we consider the five requirements for transformative learning experiences (Thompson & Zeuli, 1999) and what we learned about designing and implementing a professional development program aimed at creating "changes in deeply held beliefs, knowledge and habits of practice" (p. 342). We also suggest how reflective practice, using some of the tools and processes, can be used in other contexts. Finally, we share our learning as designers and implementers of assessment professional development.

Many of the teachers who participated in the Academy had characteristics known to be essential for effective teaching—strong content knowledge, familiarity with the ways their students struggle with learning specific content (pedagogical content knowledge), and expertise with various instructional strategies for meeting the needs of diverse learners. As a result, we were surprised to find that many teachers including some who were more experienced, began our program as relative novices with assessment. Many teachers were gauging the effectiveness of their teaching by the performance of their higher-achieving students, and they were thinking of assessment primarily as the basis for summative grades. Although most teachers knew they should pay ongoing attention to student understanding, they devoted little time to gathering and analyzing evidence systematically.

Yet as is evident throughout this book, Academy teachers transformed their practice, and the researchers on our team documented the pathways teachers took as they gained assessment expertise. Teachers were learning from each of the sections of the *ACT Portfolio* in complex and interconnected ways. Data from the researchers indicate changes in several assessment practices.

Assessment Planning

From their work on developing the Conceptual Flow and RAIM, teachers came to understand the importance of a comprehensive assessment plan. They appreciated the value of establishing clear learning goals, and they learned to identify goals more effectively. Teachers also refined their capacity to plan their assessments—to coordinate formative and summative assessments, align them with targeted learning goals, and pre-think how to use assessment data to inform their teaching. Overall, Academy teachers became critical consumers of assessments as they learned to review and refine tasks and criteria to ensure they had the tools they needed to gather appropriate evidence of student progress.

Interpreting Student Work

Academy teachers learned to look for patterns and trends in assessment data by conducting whole class and target student analysis. Learning to conceptualize scoring as more than just grading was a significant step forward as teachers came to appreciate how assessments provide critical information about student understandings of science concepts. Teachers deepened their understanding of the importance of scoring student work frequently and on a timely basis, and they learned more systematic approaches to charting and analyzing assessment data. Teachers also progressed in their capacity to make appropriate inferences from data as a way to gauge student learning and reflect on the appropriateness of unit learning goals.

Guide for Instruction

From their reflections in the "Guide for Instruction" sections of the *ACT Portfolio*, teachers expanded their ideas about instructional refinements and methods of feedback. They came to understand, for example, that while reteaching the same lesson is sometimes useful, at other times, a new experience is needed to challenge students to revise their conceptions; or it may be more appropriate to continue with the teaching sequence and revisit the concept at a later time. Many teachers also moved from thinking of feedback as only grades to thinking of it as providing students with clear information about performance and what they need to do to improve.

One outcome of the Academy was the way the portfolio process supported teachers to reflect on their assessment system for an entire instructional unit. Teachers learned the importance of the critical link between instruction and assessment and the benefits of taking ownership of their instructional materials and the assessments provided with the materials. Ownership manifested itself in a variety of contexts. For example, teachers critically reviewed unit assessments and deleted or revised unclear or biased items; developed pre-assessments, which were altogether missing in many units; and revised or developed criteria so they captured a range of student understanding. Through these activities, Academy teachers developed the understanding that assessment must be deeply integrated with instruction. As Carrie Green explained:

> *Soon after looking at the assessment, we could hardly avoid thinking about the teaching needed to reach our goal. The conversations with my teaching partner, Juan, moved us to discussions of what we could do to increase student success toward our goals. Our assessment told us what kids don't get. We now had to address what we were doing. We kept asking ourselves: What is going on in our lessons? What are we teaching? Where are we supporting their learning? How will we assess their learning next time?*

At the end of the Academy program, teachers drew pictures of their views of classroom assessment prior to CAESL, at the end of the program, and for the future and then discussed their sketches with the research team. Figure 12.1a shows Carrie's initial thinking about planning and using assessments. Carrie began with an understanding that

Figure 12.1a

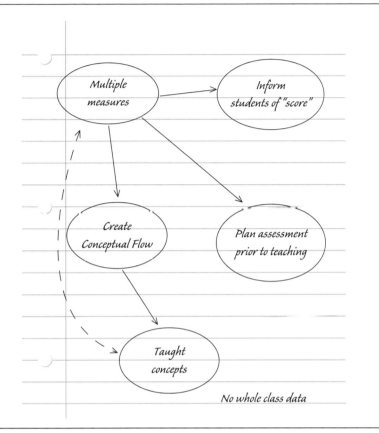

Conceptual Flows are important tools for establishing unit learning goals, but she did not use her Conceptual Flow to select her assessments. Furthermore, her conception of assessment was limited to summative assessments and "multiple measures," which provided only some information about student learning in a less than strategic way. Carrie thought of feedback as simply informing students of their scores.

After the Academy (Figure 12.1b), Carrie understood the integrated and cyclical nature of unit planning, implementation, and revision. She had come to think of assessment as a resource to guide revisions in instruction and her learning goals and to inform students of their progress throughout the unit.

As shown in Figure 12.1c, Carrie felt she still had room to grow as an assessment-centered teacher. For example, she was determined to learn how to record and analyze whole class data ("Create datasheets to focus on whole class data"), and she planned to strengthen the feedback loops within her cycle of practice in more explicit ways. (Note "analyze C.F. [Conceptual Flow] to determine if it is connecting

Figure 12.1b

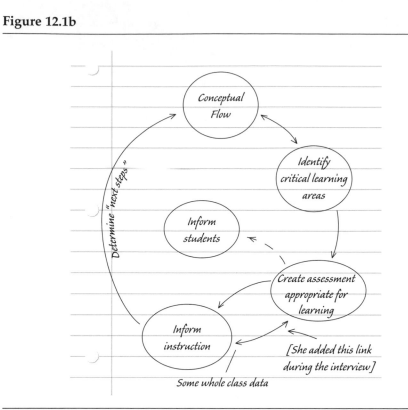

Figure 12.1c

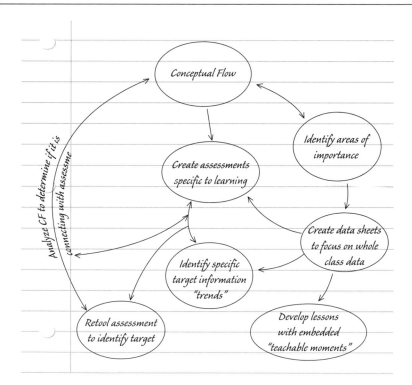

with assessments" on the left of Figure 12.1c.) These and other changes to Figure 12.1 illustrate the commitment that Carrie and the Academy teachers made to lifelong learning.

Figures 12.2a–c were drawn by a first-grade teacher, Martin Van Ness. Like many Academy teachers, Martin began with the idea (Figure 12.2a) that his responsibility was to implement a district-mandated science unit and assess his students at the conclusion of the unit before moving on to the next unit.

Figure 12.2a

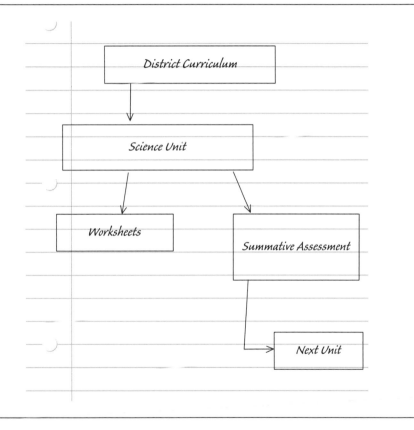

Notice how Figure 12.2b is much more complex! Through his Academy experiences and his work with Academy portfolios, Martin understood that he should plan for assessment in advance. In his drawing, he described how he identifies the learning goals and plans the assessments in detail (note all of the components in the upper half labeled "Before Teaching"). In the lower half of Figure 12.2b, he sketches multiple feedback loops to depict the ways that he uses formative assessments throughout the unit to track student progress and reteach if necessary.

Figure 12.2b

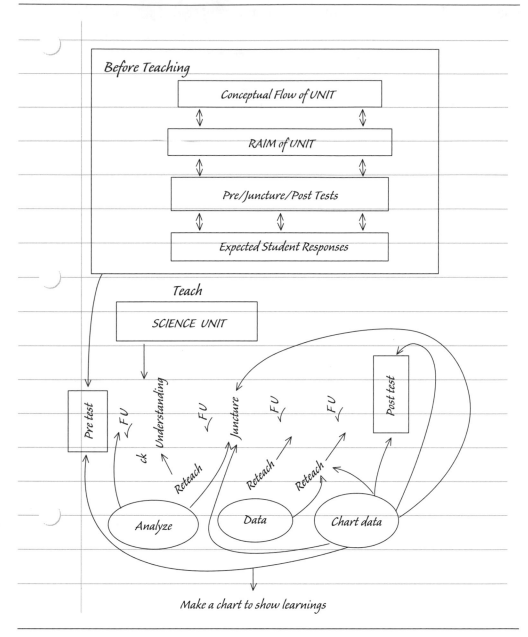

Like Carrie, he felt he had room to grow. In Figure 12.2c, he incorporated three additional ideas: align units to create a coherent yearlong science curriculum, reflect on his instruction and assessment practices throughout the unit, and analyze his assessments and refine them for next year's implementation.

Figure 12.2c

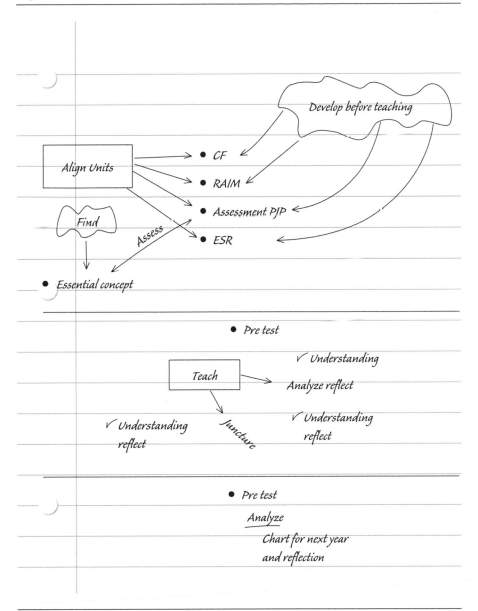

Bringing About Change in Teacher Practice: What Did We Learn?

How did these changes in practice occur? We believe that the design of the Academy activities and the *ACT Portfolio* process were key to transforming teacher knowledge, beliefs, and habits about assessment and instruction. All of the components of the *ACT Portfolio* were linked to teachers' instructional units, and our core strategy was practice based. Our portfolio process incorporated the five required elements of transformative teacher learning experiences described by Thompson and Zeuli (1999):

1. Create a high level of cognitive dissonance.

2. Provide sufficient time, structure, and support to think through the dissonance experienced.

3. Embed the dissonance creating and resolving activities in teachers' situations and practices.

4. Enable teachers to develop a new repertoire of practice that fits with their new understanding.

5. Engage teachers in a continuous process of improvement.

Below we discuss each element along with our understanding/insight about it.

1. Create a High Level of Cognitive Dissonance

The intent of this requirement is to disturb the equilibrium among teachers' existing beliefs and practices and their experience with subject matter, student learning, and teaching. Although Academy teachers were accustomed to planning activities for instruction, they tended to rely on the assessments provided in their instructional materials. Despite professed beliefs about constructivism and the learning cycle, many retained a deeply held assumption that their students "learned" what they "taught."

Building a Conceptual Flow and planning assessments through the RAIM process created dissonance for many teachers because they had to develop new ways to think about learning goals, instructional sequences, and how they would gather evidence of student learning. Writing expected student responses (ESRs), interpreting student work, and analyzing trends in student responses also prompted teachers to pay attention to student evidence in ways they had never done before. Findings from our research indicate that the portfolio repeatedly challenged teachers to wrestle with old and new ideas about assessment as they refined their approaches to constructing criteria and analyzing student responses (Gearhart et al., 2006).

In reflecting on our approach to creating this cognitive dissonance, we came to understand the following:

- *Guiding teachers to think about assessment before they launch a new unit changes the way they approach teaching.* It can change their perspective about what they are teaching, why they are teaching it, and how they will know what their students are learning. We will add one cautionary note, however. If teachers are overwhelmed with too much to learn at any given time, they are swimming in new ideas and cannot experience dissonance among old and new ideas. We found that teachers introduced to Assessment-Centered Teaching first need to be grounded in the science content of their units, reasonably familiar with their instructional materials, and knowledgeable about instructional strategies (e.g., inquiry in science) before they can experience "assessment dissonance."
- *Tensions exist between classroom assessment and large-scale assessment, especially when the two are not aligned to the same learning goals or to the same criteria for quality.* It is important to help teachers identify the tensions and balance the requirements of large-scale assessment with a formative approach to classroom assessment that can help teachers improve instruction and the conceptual understanding of their students.
- *Working together across grades K–12 provides each teacher with new and surprising perspectives.* For example, elementary teachers (who may be less confident in their understandings of science content) learn about science from their upper-grade colleagues. Secondary teachers gain new insights about pedagogy from elementary teachers, who are often inventive in the ways they engage students with hands-on activities and discussions. And of course, everyone benefits from discussions of student learning, because it is critical that teachers have an understanding of the developmental continuum across grades K–12.

2. Provide Sufficient Time, Structure, and Support to Think Through the Dissonance Experienced

The Academy provided time for both individual and collaborative reflection and structures to ensure that the time was productive. Using the *ACT Portfolio* and other processes challenged participants' thinking and required them to make sense of what they were experiencing. The support of the professional learning community was crucial for Academy teachers as they ventured into new and challenging assessment practices.

In reflecting on our approach to providing time, structure, and support, we came to understand the following:

- *Collaboration with both peers and experts is necessary to help teachers identify and resolve discrepant knowledge and beliefs.* In addition to the collaborative structures that we embedded in Academy meetings, teachers also worked on their portfolios with grade-level colleagues back at school who were implementing the same instructional units. The Academy teachers who tried out this "buddy system" reported that it was a promising strategy for resolving their uncertainties and deepening their assessment expertise.

- *Teachers who are otherwise experienced with inquiry-based science teaching may not have adequate expertise with assessment.* To strengthen their assessment practices, it is helpful to provide teachers with common experiences in collaborative teams, but when individual teachers indicate a need for differentiation, the professional development program must provide them with specialized support.

- *Interactions among teachers across grades K–12 are productive contexts for articulation.* Despite differences in context, instructional schedules, pacing, and professional cultures, our research team noted that the benefits of articulation were particularly evident when the district teams learned from each other's perspectives. This resulted in K–12 teams having the capacity to develop a systemic view of the role of assessment in science education.

- *Collaboration with assessment researchers is valuable to the professional development design, just as collaboration with scientists enriches the professional development design.* Scientists have expertise with content, and they can help us clarify appropriate learning goals, instructional strategies, and critical concepts. Assessment researchers have expertise with developing assessments and using assessment frameworks, and they can help us clarify what assessment knowledge is critical for teachers. In both cases, the interaction of the researchers and scientists with teachers is invaluable to participant learning. Relationships established through the collaboration can be long lasting and are often reciprocal.

3. Embed the Dissonance Creating and Resolving Activities in Teachers' Situations and Practices

By working with common units of instruction with the support of the *ACT Portfolio,* teachers continually reflected on the quality of their assessments, the evidence of their students' learning, and the revisions they needed to make during the course of their instruction. Interpreting student work served as a mirror for the quality of their instruction, and teachers recognized that becoming more expert with interpretation required learning new assessment concepts, such as the capacity of the assessment to capture students' alternative conceptions (Gearhart et al., 2006).

Our approach to embedding activities in teachers' situations and practices created some unexpected challenges for us. We learned the following:

- *Teachers need assessment knowledge appropriate to their contexts.* In other words, they need to focus on the content they are required to teach, the grade levels, and the characteristics of their students. Assessment knowledge cannot be learned out of context, and embedding the learning in teachers' practices resulted in depth of learning about student understanding.
- *The quality of teachers' instructional materials, including the embedded assessments, shapes teachers' opportunities to learn about assessment.* When materials have an intentional and field-tested instructional design, the student learning goals are clearly identified, and teachers are in a better position to select or design appropriate assessments for those learning goals. If the materials also provide high-quality assessments, teachers can spend more time on analysis of student work and use the results to guide instruction and provide students with feedback. However, instructional materials often fall short of the ideal, and teachers need to learn how to be critical consumers who evaluate the intent of the materials and take ownership of necessary revisions, including revisions of the assessments. Until we have quality instructional materials for all content areas at all grade levels, professional developers must help teachers use their existing instructional materials to create the best possible assessment plans.
- *Analyzing student work is different and more complex than "looking at" student work.* It requires knowledge of fundamental assessment concepts and methods, and it benefits from collaboration and a commitment to self-evaluation as well as to evaluation of

student learning. As Yogi Berra said, "You can observe a lot by watching," but observing and watching are hardly the same. The ACT Portfolio process made all the difference in getting teachers to examine and critique their assessment practices thoughtfully as well as their students' performance.

4. Enable Teachers to Develop a New Repertoire of Practices That Fits With Their New Understanding

Teachers need ongoing support to move from new understandings to changes in practice. The Academy supported those changes throughout the program by linking the *ACT Portfolio* to teachers' instructional units. One particularly productive strategy was creating the opportunity to revise a prior portfolio when implementing a unit for the second time. When teachers revised and implemented their assessment plans for the unit they were teaching a second time, they were able to apply their new understandings about assessment. Many teachers noted improvements in their students' work that resulted from revised instruction and assessment.

Our approach to enabling teachers to develop new practices that fit their new understandings led us to understand the following:

- *Transformations of teachers' knowledge and beliefs often happen in advance of changes in classroom practice.* Therefore, teachers need structured opportunities for implementation, reflection, revision, and reimplementation. Without the opportunity to apply new knowledge to practice and then reflect on practice, alignment of knowledge and beliefs with practice may never happen.

5. Engage Teachers in a Continuous Process of Improvement

Teachers involved in continuous improvement recognize that there is no end point (i.e., there is no destination, and one is never really done). The process of continuous improvement involves teachers' building on their understandings, identifying new issues that bring new understandings, and then making changes in their practices. Reflections embedded in the portfolio, coupled with opportunities to repeat the portfolio process with additional units, involved the teachers in a process of continuous improvement through reflection. When reflection became meaningful to the teachers, it became automatic, transforming their practice.

Our approach to engaging teachers in continuous improvement led us to understand the following:

- *Teachers need to be challenged to think about content in a variety of ways.* The Conceptual Flow asks teachers to apply their content knowledge to an instructional flow that meets learning goals. Interpreting student work asks teachers to think about the range of student understanding of the content and the potential presence of alternative conceptions. And revising assessment tasks and scoring criteria challenges teachers to match the content of the learning goals with the ways in which students will demonstrate their understandings.
- *Asking teachers to apply their assessment knowledge in novel ways causes them to build new understandings.* When asked to analyze the assessments in traditional instructional materials, teachers were often challenged with overcoming weaknesses in the quality of the learning sequences, specific activities, and assessments used to gauge student learning. Teachers were able to diagnose the issues and became better consumers of instructional materials and the embedded assessments.
- *Continuous improvement of reflective assessment practices requires a variety of professional development opportunities.* Through the Academy, we provided opportunities for diverse engagement with and learning of the content, including the *ACT Portfolio* process, activities, print and Web resources, and collaboration with colleagues in a variety of structures and contexts.

Application to Other Contexts

Our purpose in writing this book was to share tools and processes that we have used effectively to strengthen teachers' assessment practices. While we do not expect readers to try to replicate our professional development design, we believe that the *ACT Portfolio* and the processes we have described can be applied and used in many educational settings. The following sections provide a few suggestions for adapting the materials for your use.

Developing Professional Learning Communities

Any group of dedicated individuals who wish to pursue and deepen their learning can benefit from some version of the portfolio process. For example, a *study group* that is reviewing assessments and interpreting student work could adapt the portfolio process for team use. Our suggestion would be to start with assessments from a unit familiar to all participants and then, once grounded in the process, venture to assessments from other units. Similarly, a *lesson study group* could adapt the portfolio process when designing and evaluating a learning sequence for specific learning goals. They could use the portfolio process to interpret student work from the lesson to see if the learning goals were met. As part of an *action research project,* teachers could use the portfolio to document and evaluate their current practices and then, as they revise and refine both their instruction and assessment, they can use the portfolio to document the changes.

Instructional Materials Adoption Committees

The Conceptual Flow and the RAIM (Chapters 4 and 5) can be particularly useful for analyzing the conceptual content and organization of instructional materials as well as the quality of the assessment items. Findings from these methods would be extremely helpful to those making decisions on the quality of materials for adoption. In addition, a district that has the foresight to pilot test materials before purchasing them can use the tools for interpreting student work (Chapters 7 and 8) to evaluate the capacity of the materials to support student learning.

Preservice Education

Preservice and novice teachers need to understand that teaching requires continuous improvement throughout a career, and the portfolio provides a model and scaffold for ongoing reflection (see Taylor & Nolen, 1996). Engaging preservice teachers with processes like the Conceptual Flow and the RAIM enables them to be better consumers of instructional materials and assessment items when they join a school faculty. Having preservice teachers interpret student work using the portfolio process introduces them to habits of ongoing assessment that will serve them—and their students—well throughout their careers in education.

Instructional Materials Development

The Conceptual Flow and RAIM process can help reform-oriented materials developers to identify the appropriate placements for key assessment in an instructional unit. By mapping the content of the unit from the very outset, assessment development becomes integral to, not separate from unit development, and there is a greater likelihood that the unit activities will actually help students to understand the concepts that the assessments are designed to assess. When quality instructional materials include quality assessments that are aligned with a well-designed sequence of instructional activities, the job of teachers (and of professional developers) becomes far easier. Because superb teachers may not always be superb curriculum developers or curriculum adapters, it is important to provide teachers with the best instructional materials possible.

An End and a Beginning

We entered this work with enthusiasm for a new vision of teaching and learning focused on assessment and a commitment to understanding how teachers can strengthen their knowledge and use of assessment to support student learning. We close this chapter, knowing that like the Academy teachers, we, too, have transformed our practice—professional developers and researchers alike. We understand more deeply and completely the need for collaboration in improving the quality of teaching and learning. We have come to realize the shared responsibilities of researchers, professional developers, and school system policy makers for improving curriculum, instruction, and assessment at all levels of the educational system. We know we need to press curriculum and assessment developers to create high-quality, inquiry-based instructional materials and high-quality embedded assessments.

We understand more deeply and completely that isolated improvement often withers but that systemic, integrated improvement that transforms teacher beliefs and practice is enduring. Seeing assessment and instruction as two sides of the same coin can motivate educators to improve, and their capacity to improve requires ongoing support in terms of policy, financial commitments (for release time, substitutes, travel, materials), and day-to-day actions (e.g., avoiding practices, such as pacing guides or science kit rotations, that limit the depth and flexibility of instruction).

As professional developers, we will never again look at teaching and learning without putting assessment "front and center." As researchers, we will never again investigate the impact of professional development without documenting the collaboration and professional community that were so key to CAESL's success. As a team, we have developed insights into each other's cultures and have found true respect for each other. As Joan Herman said in the

Foreword, we have created one more bridge between theory and practice. And we intend to continue to build more.

As this book goes to press, the lessons learned from the Academy are informing a number of new initiatives. Researchers from the University of California, Los Angeles's National Center for Research on Evaluation, Standards, and Student Teaching (CRESST) and the professional development team are working with district personnel to create district benchmark assessments for fourth- and fifth-grade science. Conversations between assessment experts and school superintendents are planned to begin the dialogue about how to build and use quality assessment systems that span needs from large-scale testing to formative assessment in the classroom. Research and development projects are underway to develop higher-quality assessment tools for inquiry-based science units. Curriculum developers at the Lawrence Hall of Science are incorporating CAESL assessment practices into new curriculum projects such as Seeds of Science/Roots of Reading. These important collaborations among researchers, professional developers, curriculum developers, and district educators are crucial to the realization of our vision of Assessment-Centered Teaching.

As we progress, teachers take up our ideas and provide us the critical feedback the field needs to improve. We applaud these teachers who are eagerly building new knowledge and adopting new practices—they are making a true difference for their students by focusing on what it means to promote student learning. And, after all, our work is all about teachers and students.

Resource A

Resources for Further Learning

In this section, we suggest books that will provide you—or the teachers you work with—opportunities for further learning. These resources supplement the references that we have already cited in the text and listed in References.

Classroom Assessment—General

The resources in this section cover all aspects of classroom assessment, including technical concepts (such as reliability and validity) and their application to the classroom.

Black, Paul, Chris Harrison, Clare Lee, Bethan Marshall, and Dylan Wiliam. *Assessment for Learning: Putting It Into Practice.* Berkshire, England: Open University Press, 2004.

This book describes the learning from 36 teachers in Great Britain who, over the course of a two-year project, turned assessment for learning ideas into practical action in their school. The book provides valuable insights into the issues, successes, and problems that teachers encountered when implementing the new practices in their classrooms.

Herman, Joan, Pamela Aschbacher, and Lynn Winters. *A Practical Guide to Alternative Assessment.* Alexandria, VA: Association for Supervision and Curriculum Development, 1992.

A Practical Guide to Alternative Assessment is written for educators who are interested in creating their own alternative assessments or in understanding the issues and best methods of assessing student knowledge. The authors address topics and issues about alternative assessments, including chapters on rethinking assessment, linking assessment with instruction, determining assessment purpose, selecting assessment tasks and setting criteria, ensuring reliable scoring, and using alternative assessment for decision making. Though out of print, it is now available at www.cse.ucla.edu/CRESST/pages/products.htm.

McTighe, Jay, and Steven Ferrara. *Assessing Learning in the Classroom.* In *Student Assessment Series,* edited by Glen W. Cutlip. Annapolis Junction, MD: National Education Association, 1998.

The authors discuss principles of effective classroom assessment, describe a variety of assessment approaches, and provide a framework for planning. Teachers at all grade levels can benefit from the information.

Stiggins, Rick J. *Student-Involved Classroom Assessment.* 4th ed. Upper Saddle River, NJ: Prentice-Hall, 2006.

This book focuses on showing teachers how to develop assessments that accurately reflect student achievement and how to use those assessments to further student learning. It examines assessment topics such as articulating targets, developing quality items, and communicating results effectively—with a strong focus on integrating assessment with instruction through student involvement. The text provides guidance on how to construct all types of assessments while explaining what kinds of achievement each type can and cannot assess.

Stiggins, Rick, Judy Arter, Jan Chappuis, and Stephen Chappuis. *Classroom Assessment FOR Learning: Doing It Right, Using It Well.* Portland, OR: Educational Testing Service, 1998.

This resource is grounded in the research shown to increase student motivation and learning through improved classroom assessment. The text and accompanying workbook provide practical examples of what assessment for learning looks like in everyday instruction and suggested activities to guide teacher learning and classroom implementation. The book is formatted for use in collaborative learning teams and contains additional resources on a CD-ROM and video segments on the accompanying DVD.

Taylor, Catherine S., and Susan B. Nolen. *Classroom Assessment: Supporting Teaching and Learning in Real Classrooms.* Columbus, OH: Pearson, 2005.

This book portrays assessment as playing a central role in a teacher's everyday instruction. The authors describe how teachers can effectively use assessment to support the learning of increasingly diverse groups of students and consider the impact of assessment decisions and practices on student learning and motivation.

Wiggins, Grant. *Educative Assessment: Designing Assessments to Inform and Improve Student Performance*. San Francisco: Jossey-Bass, 1998.

Grant Wiggins outlines design principles for performance-based assessments and provides information on how to construct tasks that meet standards, score assessments fairly, and structure and judge student portfolios. The book discusses how performance assessment can be used to improve curriculum and instruction, grading, and reporting as well as teacher accountability. In addition, the book includes design templates and flowcharts and examples of assessment tasks and scoring rubrics.

Classroom Assessment—Science

These resources address several of the issues involved in assessing inquiry-based science instruction and student understanding. Several address science performance assessment tasks.

Atkin, J. Myron, and Janet E. Coffey, eds. *Everyday Assessment in the Science Classroom*. Arlington, VA: National Science Teachers Association Press, 2003.

This book is a collection of ten essays on the theories, importance, and value of formative assessment to student learning. It is designed to build confidence and enhance every teacher's ability to embed assessment into daily class work.

Atkin, J. Myron, Janet E. Coffey, S. Savitha Moorthy, Mistilina Sato, and Matthew Thibeault. *Designing Everyday Assessment in the Science Classroom*. New York: Teachers College Press, 2005.

This book is a product of the Classroom Assessment Project to Improve Teaching and Learning (CAPITAL), a research effort supported by the National Science Foundation. The book describes how middle school science teachers, in collaboration with a team of researchers, worked to improve their everyday assessment practices to enhance student learning.

Brown, Janet H., and Richard J. Shavelson. *Assessing Hands-On Science: A Teacher's Guide to Performance Assessment.* Thousand Oaks, CA: Corwin, 1996.

In a step-by-step guide, the authors provide information to help teachers choose methods that provide reliable, valid, and measurable assessment of student performance. Examples emphasize assessment of how students construct their knowledge in meaningful ways.

Keeley, Page, Francis Eberle, and Lynn Farina. *Uncovering Student Ideas in Science.* Vol. 1, *25 Formative Assessment Probes.* Arlington, VA: National Science Teachers Association, 2005.
Keeley, Page, Francis Eberle, and Lynn Farina. *Uncovering Student Ideas in Science.* Vol. 2, *25 More Formative Assessment Probes.* Arlington, VA: National Science Teachers Association, 2007.

These books provide formative assessment probes that can be used in science classrooms. The probes are supported by discussions of science content; connections to *National Science Education Standards* and *Benchmarks for Science Literacy*; developmental considerations; relevant research on learning; and instructional approaches for elementary, middle school, and high school students.

O'Brien Carlson, Maura, Gregg E. Humphrey, and Karen S. Reinhardt. *Weaving Science Inquiry and Continuous Assessment: Using Formative Assessment to Improve Learning.* Thousand Oaks, CA: Corwin, 2003.

The authors link scientific inquiry and continuous assessment to promote meaningful changes in student thinking and learning. The book provides examples of how continuous assessment, a purposeful approach to listening to and observing students, can be used to monitor and adjust inquiry-based instruction.

Price, Sabra L., and George E. Hein. *Active Assessment for Active Science: A Guide for Elementary School Teachers.* Portsmouth, NH: Heinemann, 1994.

This book combines practical discussion with theoretical information to help teachers develop and score their own assessments. The examples address assessing hands-on science in elementary classrooms.

Rubrics

These resources provide guidelines for the development of rubrics as well as examples of a variety of rubrics used for different purposes.

Ainsworth, Larry, and Jan Christinson. *Student Generated Rubrics: An Assessment Model to Help All Students Succeed.* Lebanon, IN: Dale Seymour, 1997.

This book provides a model for student-generated rubrics in grades 1–6. The book discusses methods for involving students in developing guidelines for evaluating a task, using those rubrics to complete a project, and assessing their own performance as well as the performance of their classmates.

Arter, Judith, and Jan Chappuis. *Creating and Recognizing Quality Rubrics.* Princeton, NJ: Educational Testing Service, 2006.

This book helps teachers choose or develop sound instructional rubrics, use rubrics effectively with students to maximize learning, convert rubric scores to grades, and communicate with parents about the use of rubrics in the classroom. It also includes a description of what a quality performance task looks like.

Arter, Judith, and Jay McTighe. *Scoring Rubrics in the Classroom: Using Performance Criteria for Assessing and Improving Student Performance.* Thousand Oaks, CA: Corwin Press, 2001.

This book provides guidance on how to be more consistent in judging student performance and how to help students become more effective at assessing their own learning. Examples include writing, real-world research projects, and cooperative group activities.

Alternative Conceptions in Science

These resources provide information on students' alternative conceptions in science.

Driver, Rosalind. *Children's Ideas in Science.* Buckingham, England: Open University Press, 1985.

This book documents and explores the ideas of school students (ages 10–16) about a range of natural phenomena such as light, heat, force and motion, the structure of matter, and electricity. It also examines how students' conceptions change and develop with teaching.

Driver, Rosalind, John Leach, Robin Miller, and Phil Scott. *Young People's Images of Science.* Buckingham, England: Open University Press, 1995.

The authors conducted a study of students' understanding of the nature of scientific knowledge and the relationship between science and society. This book presents the results of the study, which was conducted on students ages 9–16.

Questioning Strategies—General

This resource addresses the nuances of quality teacher-and-student and student-to-student questioning.

Walsh, Jackie A., and Beth D. Sattes. *Quality Questioning: Research-Based Practice to Engage Every Learner.* Thousand Oaks, CA: Corwin Press, 2003.

This book provides an in-depth look at how quality questions can transform classrooms. Based on 20 years of research, the authors describe strategies that engage all students in the teacher's questions and prompt students to generate their own questions.

Questioning Strategies in the Science Classroom

This resource addresses questioning in the science classroom.

Harlen, Wynne, ed. *Primary Science: Taking the Plunge.* Oxford, England: Heinemann Educational Publishers, 1985.

Harlen addresses the kinds of questions teachers ask and how teachers respond to student answers and questions. The book provides classroom examples, addresses how to develop and assess student process skills, and describes how to support students' understanding through inquiry.

Professional Development

This resource focuses on professional development that helps teachers integrate curriculum and assessment.

McTighe, Jay, and Grant Wiggins. *The Understanding by Design Professional Development Workbook.* Alexandria, VA: Association for Supervision and Curriculum Development, 2004.

This book extends the ideas presented in *Understanding by Design* (*UbD*) by focusing on professional development. The book provides information about developing curricula and assessments with a focus on deepening students' understanding.

Professional Development—Science Education

These resources address issues related specifically to professional development for quality science education.

Hazen, Robert M., and James Trefil. *Science Matters: Achieving Science Literacy.* New York: Anchor Books, 1992.

Eighteen essays address science content that the general public should know and understand. The book covers mainly life and physical science and connects the basic concepts in chemistry, physics, geology, astronomy, and biology to today's news. Although this book is over ten years old, most of the scientific concepts continue to be relevant and accurate.

Keeley, Page. *Science Curriculum Topic Study: Bridging the Gap Between Standards and Practice.* Thousand Oaks, CA: Corwin in association with the National Science Teachers Association, 2004.

Science Curriculum Topic Study links science standards and research on students' learning to curriculum, instruction, and assessment. The book provides a strategy that can be used in professional development to deepen teachers' understanding.

Rhotan, Jack, and Patricia Bowers, eds. *Issues in Science Education: Professional Development Planning and Design.* Arlington, VA: National Science Teachers Association, 2001.

This book describes the circumstances under which professional development impacts student learning, reviews programs that have been shown to be effective, and offers ideas about how professional development can sustain science education reform. The following topics are addressed: changing professional development to help with standards-based reform, building a professional development program, and using achievement data and assessment tools to modify teaching practices.

Yager, Robert E., ed. *Exemplary Science: Best Practices in Professional Development.* Arlington, VA: National Science Teachers Association, 2006.

This collection of 16 essays describes specific programs designed to support current or future teachers who seek to carry out the constructivist, inquiry-based approach of the *National Science Education Standards.* The essays describe how each professional development program works and give evidence of its effectiveness.

CAESL Partners' Web Sites

Center of Assessment and Evaluation of Student Learning (CAESL). www.caesl.org

K–12 Alliance. www.k12alliance.net; www.wested.org/cs/we/view/pj/79

University of California—Berkeley, Graduate School of Education. www-gse.berkeley.edu

University of California—Berkeley, Lawrence Hall of Science. www.lawrencehallofscience.org

University of California—Los Angeles, National Center for Research on Evaluation, Standards, and Student Testing (CRESST/UCLA). www.cse.ucla.edu

WestEd. www.wested.org

References

American Association for the Advancement of Science (AAAS). (1993). *Benchmarks for science literacy.* New York: Oxford University Press.

American Educational Research Association (AERA), American Psychological Association (APA), and National Council for Measurement in Education (NCME). (1999). *Standards for educational and psychological testing.* Washington, DC: American Educational Research Association.

Atkin, M., & Coffey, J. (Eds.). (2003). *Everyday assessment in the science classroom.* Arlington, VA: National Science Teachers Association Press.

Atkin, J. M., & Karplus, R. (1962). Discovery or invention? *Science Teacher, 29*(5), 45.

Ball, D. L. (1996). Teacher learning and the mathematics reforms: What do we think we know and what do we need to learn? *Phi Delta Kappan, 77,* 500–508.

Bass, K. M., & Glaser, R. (2004). *Developing assessments to inform teaching and learning* (CSE Report 628). Los Angeles: University of California, National Center for Research on Evaluation, Standards, and Student Testing (CRESST). (ERIC Document Reproduction Service No. ED483395)

Biological Sciences Curriculum Studies (BSCS). (2003). *BSCS biology: A human approach* (2nd ed.). Dubuque, IA: Kendall Hunt.

Black, P., Harrison, C., Lee, C., Marshall, B., & Wiliam, D. (2003). *Assessment for learning: Putting it into practice.* Maidenhead Berkshire, England: Open University Press.

Black, P., & Wiliam, D. (1998a). Assessment and classroom learning. *Assessment in Education, 5,* 70–74.

Black, P., & Wiliam, D. (1998b). Inside the black box: Raising standards through classroom assessment. *Phi Delta Kappan, 80,* 139–148.

Bransford, J. D., Brown, A. L., & Cocking, R. R. (Eds.). (1999). *How people learn.* Washington, DC: National Academy Press.

Bybee, R. W. (1997). *Achieving scientific literacy: From purposes to practices.* Portsmouth, NH: Heinemann.

California Department of Education. (2000). *Science content standards for California public schools: Kindergarten through grade twelve.* S. Bruton, F. Ong, & G. Geeting (Eds.). Sacramento, CA: Author.

Craig, J., Butler, A., Cairo, L., Wood, C., Gilchrist, C., Holloway, J., Williams, S., & Moats, S. (2005). *A case study of six high-performing schools in Tennessee.* Charleston, WV: Appalachia Educational Laboratory (AEL) at Edvantia.

Cuff, K. (with Carmichael, I., & Willard, C.). (2002). *Great Explorations in Math and Science (GEMS). Plate tectonics: The way the earth works.* University of California—Berkeley, Lawrence Hall of Science.

Davis, E. A., & Krajcik, J. S. (2005). Designing educative curriculum materials to promote teacher learning. *Educational Researcher, 34*(3), 3–14.

DiRanna, K. (Ed.). (1989). *What's the big idea training manual,* Unpublished manuscript. Irvine, CA: California Science Implementation Network.

DiRanna, K., & Cerwin, K. (1994). Decision point assessments. In K. DiRanna (Ed.), *What's the big idea training manual,* Unpublished manuscript. Irvine, CA: California Science Implementation Network.

DiRanna, K., & Topps, J. (2004, September). Going with the flow. *What's the big idea? A publication of the K–12 alliance: A WestEd program, 4*(1), 1–2, 4.

Donovan, M. S., Bransford, J. D., & Pellegrino, J. W. (Eds.). (1999). *How people learn: Bridging research and practice.* Washington, DC: National Academy Press.

Driver, R., Squires, A., Rushworth, P., & Wood-Robinson, V. (1994). *Making sense of secondary science: Research into children's ideas.* London: Routledge.

Edgerton, R., Hutchings, P., & Quinlan, K. (1991). *The teaching portfolio: Capturing the scholarship in teaching.* Washington, DC: American Association for Higher Education.

Full Option Science System (FOSS) Diversity of Life Middle School Course, Teacher Guide. (2003). Nashua, NH: Delta Education. (Developed at the Lawrence Hall of Science, University of California—Berkeley).

Full Option Science System (FOSS) Earth Materials Module, Teacher Guide. (2001) Nashua, NH: Delta Education. (Developed at the Lawrence Hall of Science, University of California—Berkeley).

Fuchs, L. S., & Fuchs, D. (1986). Effects of systematic formative evaluation: A meta-analysis. *Exceptional Children, 53*(3), 199–208.

Gearhart, M., Nagashima, S., Pfotenhauer, J., Clark, S., Schwab, C., Vendlinski, T., Osmundson, E., Herman, J., & Bernbaum, D. J. (2006). Developing expertise with classroom assessment in K–12 science: Learning to interpret student work; Interim findings from a 2-year study. *Educational Assessment, 11*(3/4), 237–263.

Herman, J. L. (1997). Assessing new assessments: How do they measure up? *Theory Into Practice, 36,* 196–204.

Hord, S. (1998). Creating a professional learning community: Cottonwood Creek School. Washington, DC: Office of Educational Research and Improvement. (ERIC Document Reproduction Service No. ED424685)

Karplus, R., & Thier, H. (1967). *A new look at elementary school science.* Chicago: Rand McNally.

Kennedy, C. A., Brown, N. J. S., Draney, K., & Wilson, M. (2005, April). *Using progress variables and embedded assessments to improve teaching and learning.* Paper presented at the annual meeting of the American Educational Research Association (AERA), Montreal, Canada.

Knowles, M., Holton, E., & Swanson, R. (1998). *The adult learner.* Woburn, MA: Butterworth-Heinemann.

Little, J., Gearhart, M., Curry, M., & Kafka, J. (2003). Looking at student work for teacher learning, teacher community and school reform. *Phi Delta Kappan, 85,* 184–192.

Loucks-Horsley, S., Love, N., Stiles, K. E., Mundry, S., & Hewson, P. W. (2003). *Designing professional development for teachers of science and mathematics* (2nd ed.). Thousand Oaks, CA: Corwin Press.

Louis, K. S., Kruse, S., & Bryk, T. (Eds.). (1995). *Professionalism and community.* Thousand Oaks, CA: Corwin Press.

Marzano, R. (2001). *Classroom instruction that works: Research based strategies for improving student achievement.* Alexandria, VA: Association for Supervision and Curriculum Development.

McLaughlin, M., & Talbert, J. (2001). *Professional communities and the work of high school teaching.* Chicago: University of Chicago Press.

National Board for Professional Teaching Standards. (2001). *The impact of National Board Certification on teachers: A survey of National Board Certified Teaching and Assessors.* Arlington, VA: Author.

National Research Council (NRC). (1996). *National science education standards.* Washington DC: National Academy Press.

National Research Council (NRC). (1999). *Designing mathematics or science curriculum programs: A guide for using mathematics and science education standards.* Washington, DC: National Academy Press.

National Research Council (NRC). (2001). *Classroom assessment and the national science education standards.* Washington DC: National Academy Press.

National Science Resources Center. (2000). *Science and Technology Concepts for Middle Schools (STC/MS). Properties of matter.* Burlington, NC: Carolina Biological Supply Company (CBSC).

National Science Resources Center. (2003). *Science and Technology Concepts for Middle Schools (STC/MS). Organisms—From Macro to Micro.* Burlington, NC: Carolina Biological Supply Company (CBSC).

National Staff Development Council. (2001). *Standards for staff development* (Rev. ed.) [Electronic version]. Retrieved 2004 from www.nsdc.org/standards/index.cfm

Osterman, K. F., & Kottkamp, R. B. (2004). *Reflective practice for educators.* Thousand Oaks, CA: Corwin Press.

Pellegrino, J., Chudowsky, N., & Glaser, R. (Eds.) (Committee on the Foundations of Assessment under the aegis of Board on Testing and Assessment, Center for Education, Division of Behavioral and Social Science and Education, National Research Council). (2001). *Knowing what students know: The science and design of educational assessment.* Washington, DC: National Academy Press.

44444444

444444444

Plake, B. S., & Impara, J. C. (1997). Teacher assessment literacy: What do teachers know about assessment? In G. Phye (Ed.), *Handbook of classroom assessment* (pp. 53–68). San Diego, CA: Academic Press.

Popham, W. J. (2008). *Classroom assessment: What teachers need to know* (5th ed.). Boston: Pearson, Allyn and Bacon.

Reagan, T. G., Case, C., & Brubacher, J. (2000). *Becoming a reflective educator: How to build a culture of inquiry in the schools* (2nd ed.). Thousand Oaks, CA: Corwin Press.

Schön, D. (1983). *The reflective practitioner.* New York: Basic Books.

Shavelson, R., Ruiz-Primo, M. A., & Wiley, E. (2005) Windows into the mind. *Higher Education, 49,* 413–440.

Shepard, L. A. (2001). The role of classroom assessment in teaching and learning. In V. Richardson (Ed.), *The handbook of research on teaching* (4th ed., pp. 1066–1101). Washington, DC: American Educational Research Association.

Shulman, L. (1998). *Teacher portfolios: A theoretical activity.* In N. Lyons (Ed.), *With portfolio in hand.* (pp. 23–37). New York: Teachers College Press.

Shulman, L. (1986). Those who understand: Knowledge growth in teaching. *Educational Researcher, 15*(2), 4–14.

Stiggins, R. J. (2002). Assessment crisis: The absence of assessment FOR learning. *Phi Delta Kappan, 83,* 758–765.

Taylor, C. S., & Nolen, S. B. (1996). A contextualized approach to teaching teachers about classroom-based assessment. *Educational Psychologist, 31,* 77–88.

Thompson, C. L., & Zeuli, J. S. (1999). The frame and tapestry: Standards-based reform and professional development. In L. Darling-Hammond & G. Sykes (Eds.), *Teaching as the learning profession: Handbook of policy and practice* (pp. 341–375). San Francisco: Jossey-Bass.

Weiss, I. R. (1997). The status of science and mathematics teaching in the United States: Comparing teacher views and classroom practice to national standards. *NISE* (National Institute for Science Education) *Brief 1*(3), 1–7. (ERIC Document Reproduction Service No. ED411158)

Wiggins, G., & McTighe, J. (2005). *Understanding by design.* Alexandria, VA: Association for Supervision and Curriculum Development.

Wilson, M. (2004). *Constructing measures: An item response modeling approach.* Mahwah, NJ: Erlbaum.

Wolf, D. (1994). Curriculum and assessment standard: Common measures or conversations? In Cobb, N. (Ed.), *The future of education: Perspectives on national standards in America* (p. 88). New York: College Entrance Examination Board.

Wolf, K., & Dietz, M. (1998). Teaching portfolios: Purposes and possibilities. *Teacher Education Quarterly, 25,* 9–22.

York-Barr, J., Sommers, W. A., Ghere, G. S., & Montie, J. K. (2001). *Reflective practice to improve schools: An action guide for educators.* Thousand Oaks, CA: Corwin Press.

Index

CORWIN PRESS

WestEd